MERRIAM CENTER LIBRARY
AMERICAN PLANNING ASSOCIATION

Visions of Urban Excellence

1997
Rudy Bruner Award for Urban Excellence

Jay Farbstein, PhD, FAIA
Richard Wener, PhD
Emily Axelrod, MCP

Bruner Foundation, Inc.

Library of Congress Catalog Card Number: 98-071243
ISBN: 1-890286-02-8

© Copyright 1998 by the Bruner Foundation
130 Prospect St.
Cambridge, MA 02139

All rights reserved. No part of this book may be reproduced, stored in a retrieval system, or transmitted in any form or by any means, electronic, mechanical, photocopying, microfilming, recording or otherwise, without written permission from the publisher.

Contents

  v   **Preface**

 vii   **Introduction**   The Rudy Bruner Award for Urban Excellence

  1   **Gold Medal Winner**   The Times Square, New York, New York

 23   **Silver Medal Winner**   Project Row Houses, Houston, Texas

 47   **Silver Medal Winner**   Hismen Hin-nu, Oakland, California

 67   **Silver Medal Winner**   Center in the Square, Roanoke, Virginia

 87   **Silver Medal Winner**   Cleveland Historic Warehouse District, Cleveland, Ohio

107   **What Was Learned About Urban Excellence**
      Vision (109)
      Art in the City (111)
      Quality of Place (114)
      Preservation as a Strategy for Change (116)
      Public/Private Collaboration (119)
      Adapting New Models of Urban Placemaking (121)
      Sustaining Urban Excellence (122)
      Conclusion (124)

Preface

It is a pleasure for me to introduce the sixth round of the Rudy Bruner Award. The five winners are very different, one from the other, and exemplify the kinds of places that imagination and hard work can create.

When we started the Rudy Bruner Award twelve years ago, our original plan was to cease operation in ten years. We assumed that the issues would have been fully described within five award cycles. We knew that in designing the Award, it was critical to provide a clear framework, but one which would allow for each Selection Committee to define its own priorities and criteria. This would ensure that the Award would stay current over time in dealing with the important issues which affect our nations' cities. We did not know at the time how successful this strategy would be, and it has been gratifying to see in our winners the emergence of new, creative approaches to some of our cities' most critical problems. I know when you read about The Times Square, Project Row Houses, Center in the Square, the Cleveland Warehouse District, and Hismen Hin-Nu, you will be equally impressed. In each of them, a group of hardworking, dedicated citizens and professionals has pursued a vision of what could and should be done — in some cases against very significant odds — and turned their visions into dynamic projects which make important contributions to their urban contexts. I am sure it would be their fondest hope that you learn from their experience and use it in your own communities.

As we talk about these winners, I am constantly amazed at how well they have taken an idea — sometimes a new idea, and sometimes a reinvention of an old idea — and re-worked it to relate to their unique urban settings. The size of The Times Square, for example, is an advantage in New York City, allowing it to create a social service structure at a significant enough scale to impact the homeless and disenfranchised population. In a smaller town, its size and the concentration of needy population might be a disadvantage.

We would be wise to learn from the creative strategies designed for the management of this socially complex project — specifically, the successful mix of tenant populations and the interplay between social services and building management — when considering this model. Each of the 1997 winners may provide innovative and useful models for your city. That is not to suggest that one should simply attempt to replicate these projects, but rather take what is useful, creative, and effective, and adapt it to the uniqueness of your urban setting.

It is the creativity and appropriateness with which one adapts pre-existing models to create new and unique solutions that allows us to move forward. Many of these models, including The Times Square, Project Row Houses, and Center in the Square, are already being adapted in other cities, either by their original founders, or by others who have learned from them.

We at the Rudy Bruner Award hope that these exciting urban places will provide you with some food for thought, and with some potential solutions to the problems facing your own cities. They teach us how to identify strengths in even the most troubled urban settings, and to build upon those strengths to enhance the urban environment. They are examples of what can be done, and perhaps more importantly, of what you can do. We encourage you to use these winners as resources for the hard work of creating excellent urban places. Good luck!

Simeon Bruner, Founder

Introduction

The Rudy Bruner Award

The Rudy Bruner Award for Urban Excellence seeks to discover and to celebrate urban places which reflect the successful integration of thoughtful processes and meaningful values into good design. In this search, the award serves as a national forum for debating urban issues and the nature of urban excellence. The Rudy Bruner Award is distinguished from other award programs by its broadly representative Selection Committee (which meets for two full days, and is composed of mayors, community representatives, elected officials, design professionals and developers); its comprehensive application process (which requires statements from a range of involved parties, not just the owner and designer); and the in-depth site visits to each finalist.

Our current and past winners are a diverse group of places which lend vitality to the neighborhoods in which they are located. Some represent new models of urban placemaking guided by creative visions of what is possible, often in defiance of existing norms. They may be guided by leaders whose imagination and creativity fostes new ways of thinking about the urban environment. Others reflect complex collaborations among people who represent different perspectives and sectors of society. In learning about these unique places, we discover creative solutions to some of our most intractable urban problems.

The Rudy Bruner Award is an ongoing exploration into the nature of urban excellence. In the context of the applications, each Selection Committee is called upon to address and debate the factors that make an excellent urban place. What kinds of places make our cities better places to live, work, and play? Which projects enhance the urban environment and at the same time provide safe, attractive, and welcoming spaces for the complex interactions of urban life? How do these places come into being? What makes them succeed? How are they sustained? The Rudy Bruner Award looks closely at the complex set of interactions whereby projects balance opportunity with cost; form with use; and tradition with change.

Eligibility Criteria

The award seeks excellence in places where it may not be expected. Eligibility criteria are therefore broadly defined. The minimum criteria are:

- The project must be a real place, not just a plan. It must be able to demonstrate its excellence when visited.
- The project must be located in the United States. Site visits are integral to the award process, and it is not feasible to conduct visits at international locations.

The Selection Process

A new Selection Committee is appointed for each award cycle. It meets twice, first to select the five winners from a field of about 100 applications, and later to select the Gold Medal Winner. Between the two meetings, Bruner Foundation staff makes a two- or three-day site visit to every finalist, to answer questions raised by the Selection Committee and to explore the project more thoroughly. The Foundation representatives serve as the Selection Committee's eyes and ears, touring all parts of the project, interviewing participants, taking photographs, and observing patterns of use.

After the site visits the Foundation prepares a report and slide show for the second Selection Committee meeting, where the 5 finalists are reviewed in depth. At this second meeting, the Selection Committee debates the merits of each project, and in so

Introduction

1997 Rudy Bruner Award for Urban Excellence

doing explores and deepens our understanding of urban excellence. This discussion determines which project will be the Gold Medal winner and receive $50,000, and which will be Silver Medal winners and receive $10,000.

The dialogue at the Selection Committee level is at the heart of the Rudy Bruner Award. Each Selection Committee includes a mayor of a major American city and urban experts from the fields of architecture, finance, development, community organization, and philanthropy. Because the Selection Committee is always composed of a group of distinguished experts on the urban environment, their discussions become a forum for exploring the issues confronting American cities and the solutions being tested around the country. Also, because there are no pre-established criteria for evaluating applications, the Selection Committee must develop criteria on the basis of their own expertise and knowledge of the issues facing our cities today.

The 1997 Selection Committee

Hon. Kurt L. Schmoke, *Mayor of Baltimore, Maryland*

Robert Curvin, *Vice President for Communications, Ford Foundation, New York*

Roberta Feldman, Ph.D., *City Design Center, University of Illinois, Chicago*

Susan Rice, *formerly of Fleet Bank, N.A. New Jersey*

Robert M. Weinberg, *Chairman, MarketPlace Development, and President, Friends of Post Office Square, Boston. (The Park at Post Office Square was a 1993 Rudy Bruner Award winner.)*

Selection Criteria

The criteria put forward by this year's committee were:

Entrepreneurial Vision

- Does the project demonstrate entrepreneurial leadership by finding new ways to implement visionary thinking?
- Is there a significant vision that informs the project?
- Did that vision result in a worthy outcome?

Uniqueness

- Is the project unusual or special within its context?
- Does it have something new or important to teach us?

Hon. Kurt L. Schmoke

Robert Curvin

Roberta Feldman, Ph.D.

Susan Rice

Robert M. Weinberg

Community Impact
- Does the project have a significant positive impact on its immediate neighborhood or the broader community?
- Did the project identify and address a problem that might not otherwise have been addressed?
- How does it contribute to civic learning?

Sustainability
- Does the project have the ability to sustain itself over time?

Cost Effectiveness
- Does the project demonstrate an effective use of available funds?
- Has it harnessed funds that might have gone elsewhere?

Creation of Place
- Is the project a quality place? Is it well designed? Of quality materials?
- How does the project impact people's perceptions of the neighborhood? The community?

Values
- Are the values and goals for the project made explicit?
- Were those values realized and sustained through the development process?
- Were the risks and impacts of gentrification considered?

Replicability
- Does the project represent a model that can be meaningfully adapted to other settings?
- Could the process, or aspects of the process, be adapted in other cities?

Reflecting the Essence of the Urban Setting
- Does the project recognize what is special and unique about its setting, and build upon it?

Using these criteria, the 1997 Selection Committee selected The Times Square as the Gold Medal winner, and Project Row Houses, Cleveland Historic Warehouse District, Hismen Hin-nu (Sun Gate) Terrace, and Center in the Square as Silver Medal winners.

The 1997 Rudy Bruner Award Winners

The Times Square A derelict hotel in the heart of Times Square, New York, had become a microcosm of the social problems that plague many urban areas. Common Ground Community HDFC, Inc., together with Center for Urban Community Services, saw the potential for the rehabilitation of this notorious hotel, and for providing dignified housing for a neglected population. The Times Square now provides permanent, affordable single room occupancy housing for 652 adults. Some of the residents had been homeless, others are HIV-positive or suffer from mental or emotional problems, and some are low-income adults seeking permanent housing. In defiance of prior norms for this type of housing, The Times Square has brought this mixed population together at an unprecedented scale, to form a stable community with on-site social service support and job training. In so doing, the Times Square has created a new model for combining SRO housing, social service delivery, and job training, at the same time rehabilitating an architecturally significant historic building.

Project Row Houses The preservation of 22 historic "shotgun" houses and their transformation into art gallery space in Houston's Third Ward has changed a neglected neighborhood adjacent to downtown Houston into a new destination for Houston residents. Project Row Houses is an innovative concept based upon the power of art to transform a community. At Project Row

Introduction

1997 Rudy Bruner Award for Urban Excellence

Houses, well known African-American artists install their work in eight gallery houses, and interact with the community. Project Row Houses has several other significant programs in place, including the Young Mothers Residential Program, which provides houses to young women for a period of one year while they receive training and support for parenting, education, and job skills.

Hismen Hin-nu (Sun Gate Terrace) A mixed use project in Oakland, California, Hismen Hin-nu used a hands-on participatory process to involve the community in planning and design. Located in the heart of the racially and socially diverse San Antonio community, Hismen Hin-nu offers varied configurations of affordable housing units and street-level retail space. Its architecture is based upon California's historic Mission style, and incorporates multi-cultural art themes, including the symbolic Sun Gate, designed by a local artist and located at the entrance to the project.

Center in the Square The Center brought together five major cultural institutions into a destination arts complex in downtown Roanoke, Virginia. Center in the Square provides rent-free space to these institutions, promoting synergy among the cultural institutions and with the adjacent farmers' market. The project has contributed to the revitalization of downtown Roanoke, especially the adjacent market area, and provides an educational and cultural resource to Western Virginia.

Cleveland Historic Warehouse District The Warehouse District has been successful in preserving a series of vacant Victorian warehouses in the heart of downtown Cleveland, Ohio, and in transforming them into a new urban neighborhood with over 1,500 units of housing and a variety of commercial uses. Adjacent to the center of downtown, this new neighborhood preserves Cleveland's urban fabric, and introduces life and activity during the day and evening hours, strengthening and diversifying the downtown area, and preserving an irreplaceable architectural resource.

Award Presentation

Since the goal of the Rudy Bruner Award is to celebrate urban excellence, the presentation ceremonies are an important part of the award process. For the 1997 winners, award presentations were made in September, at press conferences held in each winner's city. The presentations attracted mayors, city officials, design and planning professionals, community leaders, tenants, community organizers, and community residents, who spoke about the meaning of these projects to their communities.

The presentation of the Gold Medal award to The Times Square featured remarks by Gordon Campbell, Commissioner for Homelessness in New York; Gretchen Dykstra, President of the Times Square Business Improvement District; and Robert Curvin, Vice President for Communications at the Ford Foundation, and member of the 1997 Rudy Bruner Award Selection Committee.

Gorden Campbell, Commissioner for Homelessness in New York, speaking at The Times Square Award Presentation.

Robert Curvin, 1997 Selection Committee, speaking at The Times Square Award Presentation.

Mr. Campbell spoke forcefully about the importance of The Times Square in providing a new and effective model for dealing with homelessness in New York. Ms. Dykstra spoke about the contribution of the project to stabilization of a major corner in the heart of the Times Square Business Improvement District. Mr. Curvin represented the 1997 Selection Committee in commending the innovative thinking which characterizes The Times Square and the significance of this new model for dealing with homelessness, affordable housing, and effective job training.

The Rudy Bruner Award and its winners have been recognized in past award presentations by the U.S. Conference of Mayors, the U.S. Department of Housing and Urban Development, and the Environmental Design Research Association (EDRA), as well as in *Places, Designer/Builder, Design Book Review,* and *Casabella* magazines.

Simeon Bruner presenting The 1997 Rudy Bruner Award to Rosanne Haggerty of The Times Square.

About This Book

The Bruner Foundation is committed to the process of learning about urban excellence, and to continuing to ask the question, "What is an excellent urban place?" The purpose of the Rudy Bruner Award books is to make the dialogue and debate among the Selection Committee members and the innovative thinking of the winners available to policy makers and practitioners across the country.

This book presents the 1997 winners in the context of the Selection Committee discussion on the nature of urban excellence, and of the criteria they developed. Detailed case studies of each 1997 winner are included. The case studies are based upon the site visits conducted in the winter of 1997 and the Selection Committee discussion about each place. Selection Committee comments are summarized at the beginning of each chapter in the section entitled "Project at a Glance." The book concludes with a chapter about "What Was Learned About Urban Excellence," which presents the following themes:

- Vision
- Art in the City
- Quality of Place
- Preservation as a Strategy for Change
- Public Private Collaboration
- Adapting New Models of Urban Placemaking
- Sustaining Urban Excellence

Publications

At the conclusion of each award cycle, the Bruner Foundation publishes a book documenting the Selection Committee discussion on urban excellence, and describing detailed case studies of

xi

each Rudy Bruner Award winner. The publications, some of which are available from the Bruner Foundation, include:

- *Urban Excellence*, by Philip Langdon with Robert Shibley and Polly Welch; Van Nostrand Reinhold, 1990.
- *Breakthroughs: Re-creating the American City*, by Neil Pierce and Robert Guskind; Center for Urban Policy Research, Rutgers University, 1993.
- *Connections: Creating Urban Excellence*, by Jay Farbstein and Richard Wener; Bruner Foundation, 1992.
- *Rebuilding Communities: Re-Creating Urban Excellence*, by Jay Farbstein and Richard Wener; Bruner Foundation, 1993.
- *Building Coalitions for Urban Excellence*, by Jay Farbstein and Richard Wener; Bruner Foundation, 1995.

A recent Bruner Foundation endeavor has allowed us to revisit the winners and finalists from the first four cycles of the award to learn how the projects have fared over time. In examining which have continued to thrive and which have struggled, some important conclusions were drawn about sustaining urban excellence. Partially funded by a grant from the U.S. Department of Housing and Urban Development, 21 projects were revisited by teams of foundation staff and consultants, HUD regional staff, and past Selection Committee members. The book is available through the Bruner Foundation:

- *Sustaining Urban Excellence; Learning from the Rudy Bruner Award, 1987–1993*, by Jay Farbstein, Robert Shibley, Polly Welch, and Richard Wener, with Emily Axelrod, Bruner Foundation, 1998.

Access To Rudy Bruner Award Materials

- All Rudy Bruner Award applications have been recorded on microfiche and are accessible through the Interlibrary Loan Department of the Lockwood Memorial Library at the State University of New York at Buffalo, Amherst, NY 14260. Phone: 716-636-2816. Fax: 716-636-3721.
- An abstract and key word identification has been prepared for each application, and can be accessed through two major data bases: RLIN/Research Library Information Network, and OCLF/First Search.
- The State University of New York at Buffalo maintains a web site with 1995 and 1997 Rudy Bruner Award applicants. A portion of the applications have been posted to date. The web site address is: http://wings.buffalo.edu/libraries/projects/digital/bruner
- A complete Bruner Foundation archive is maintained at the University of Indiana library.
- The Rudy Bruner Award web site address is: www.brunerfoundation.org.

gold MEDAL 1997

The Times Square
New York, New York

THE TIMES SQUARE

The Times Square At A Glance

What is The Times Square?

- A 652 unit supportive housing facility for formerly homeless and low income adults, elderly, mentally ill, and persons with HIV/AIDS.
- Ground floor commercial space rented to three retail operations that support job training and hiring programs.

Who Made the Submission?

- Common Ground Community HDFC, Inc./T.S. Hotel Limited Partnership.

Major Goals of The Times Square

- To restore an historic but dilapidated hotel without displacing 200+ residents;
- To "address homelessness and joblessness through the creation of innovative programs designed to promote stability and independence;"
- To provide decent, permanent housing for low income adults, people with mental and physical disabilities, or AIDS;
- To convert a building that was a "trouble spot" on an already difficult block to one that supports and promotes the renewal of Times Square;
- To provide a model for successful, large scale single room occupancy (SRO) hotels in an urban context.

Major Accomplishments of The Times Square

- Completion of a high quality restoration of the hotel, preserving and restoring original architectural features;
- Providing 652 units of secure and supportive permanent housing;
- Providing a wide range of social services to maintain the independence of the residents;

The Times Square, New York, prior to renovation.

- Inclusion of an economic development program, which provides training and placement of residents in jobs in building operations, the retail shops located in the facility, and other corporate settings;
- Demonstration of the feasibility of large scale SROs, affordable housing, and delivery of high quality social services and economic development programs in a cost-effective manner.

Reasons for Including The Times Square as a Finalist

- It provides housing for a population that might otherwise be displaced by high rent investments in the area.
- Common Ground looked closely at internal design issues and paid attention to user needs.
- The facility demonstrates good contextual design through the renovation of an historic structure to provide an attractive living environment and enhance streetscape continuity.

Selection Committee Questions and Concerns for Site Visit

- What is the population in the building and how does it work? Do people get along or are there conflicts and antagonisms?
- What sort of changes do people living in the building experience in their own life cycles (e.g., how many move "up" and out to other permanent housing; how many drift back to the streets)?
- What are the social services offered in the building? To what level are they utilized (number of residents, content, quality, contact hours)? Are services adequate? How are they funded and how stable is the funding (is it endowed or capitalized)?
- What was the design process? Were the residents involved in the design? Was anyone involved who was sensitive to or knowledgeable about this group's needs?
- What is the quality of the design and of materials?
- Has any follow-up been done on how design relates to resident satisfaction?
- What is the organization for managing the building? Is there self-management? Are residents involved? Are maintenance activities and budgets adequate?
- How do neighbors view the project (shop owners, property owners and developers)?
- Does the project have any relationship to the major renewal of the Times Square neighborhood?

Final Selection Committee Comments

- The Committee felt that The Times Square demonstrated high standards of historic renovation, while providing exceptionally high quality affordable housing.
- The Times Square used an "entrepreneurial approach" to "create an effective instrument" to address the serious unmet needs of this population.
- The Times Square provides a model for other facilities and other cities in terms of the scale of the project, the mix of population, and the services involved.

Project Description

Project Chronology

May, 1990 Rosanne Haggerty begins exploring a supportive housing concept for The Times Square with service providers, advocates and not-for-profit developers.

June, 1990 43rd St. Development Corporation, holder of first mortgage, assumes control of The Times Square Hotel when there are no bidders at the bankruptcy auction of its property, and begins to work with Haggerty to explore supportive housing plans.

Summer, 1990 Haggerty and team meet with city agencies, community representatives, and local business people to create and refine proposal. Final plan is circulated in September.

Fall, 1990 Plan is reviewed and modified in further meetings with city and community groups. Common Ground incorporates and applies for tax exempt status.

November, 1990 City conditionally approves $28 million SRO development loan.

December, 1990 Community Boards overwhelmingly vote in favor of Common Ground proposal (rejecting private developer's bid to create tourist hotel). Low income tax credit allocation obtained.

January, 1991 Common Ground plan approved by Mayor Dinkins and development loan is authorized.

March, 1991 Common Ground closes on acquisition of The Times Square Hotel.

Spring, 1991 102 tenants are relocated from east to west side of building for renovation. Some rooms are cosmetically upgraded to make relocation possible. Common Ground holds discussions with tenants on service delivery. First construction bids come in.

July–October, 1991 Remaining occupied rooms upgraded. Section 8 vouchers introduced for eligible tenants. New construction bids obtained.

November, 1991 Construction begins on east side of the building.

Winter, 1992 Unions demand use of union workers and wages, and begin to picket construction site (resolved by National Labor Relations Board and courts in March).

Spring, 1992 Begin tenant employment program, hiring tenants for desk, security, maintenance, clerical jobs.

April, 1992 Common Ground decides to pursue tax credits for historic restoration.

September, 1992 Begin marketing and intake for new tenants.

February, 1993 East side construction completed and first tenants move in. Begin relocating original tenants to newly rehabilitated rooms (completed in May).

May, 1993 Phase I (east side) fully rented, construction on west side (Phase II) begins. Social service programs intensified to integrate new and original tenants.

April, 1994 Ben & Jerry's opens in ground floor retail space.

May, 1994 Phase II completed, some original tenants moved back to west side. Fully occupied by June.

August, 1994 New 15th floor dining and kitchen completed, mezzanine and lobby refurbishing finished.

Key Participants *(persons interviewed are indicated by an asterisk*)*

Rosanne Haggerty,* *Executive Director, Common Ground*
Tony Hannigan,* *Executive Director, Center for Urban Community Services*
Dennis White,* *Metropolitan Life Foundation*
Bill Daly,* *Mayor's Office of Midtown Enforcement*
Paul Parkhill, *Housing Development Director, Common Ground*
Jennifer Smith,* *Economic Development Assistant, Common Ground*
John Weiler,* *Economic Development Director, Common Ground*
Justine Zinkin, *Job Placement Director, Common Ground Tenants*
Ed Simmons,* tenant
Antoinette Jones,* tenant
Patricia Cassisa,* tenant
David Deblinger,* tenant
Linda Parish,* tenant

Designers
Elise Quasebarth,* *Historic Preservation Consultant*
Liz Newman,* *Architect, Beyer, Blinder, Belle*

City
Fran Reiter,* *Former Deputy Mayor*

Tim O'Hanlon,* *New York City Housing Preservation and Development*
David Klasfeld,* *Former Chief of Staff, Office of Deputy Mayor, New York City*
Jack Goldstein,* *Former Chair, Community Board 5*

Others
Gretchen Dykstra,* *President, Times Square Business Improvement District*
Janelle Ferris, *Director of Community Services, Times Square Business Improvement District*
Rebecca Robertson,* *Former President, 42nd St. Development Project*
A. O. Sulzberger, Jr.,* *Chairman, New York Times*
Several hotel managers and store owners in Times Square*

Organization

Two organizations — Common Ground and the Center for Urban Community Services (CUCS) — are responsible for the development and operation of The Times Square. Common Ground, as the developer, is responsible for all building-related operations, including maintenance and security and economic development efforts, such as leasing retail space, and for finding outside job placements for residents. Common Ground has taken as its partner CUCS, which handles all social services, including intake interviews, benefits advocacy, and vocational counseling. The two organizations coordinate well and work together closely. CUCS and Common Ground jointly determine acceptance of new residents. Common Ground looks to CUCS social workers to help with problem tenants, through counseling, substance abuse programs, etc. CUCS helps residents identify vocational goals and possibilities, works with them to get the necessary training and education, and then refers them to Common Ground for job placement. Common Ground's economic development plan works to create job opportunities through the use of its ground floor retail space, and through relationships with outside employers.

Rosanne Haggerty of Common Ground

City officials and others with whom we spoke thought that this bifurcation of responsibilities was a critical part of the success of The Times Square model. Gretchen Dykstra, of The Times Square Business Improvement District, feels that CUCS and Common Ground often act as "good cop/bad cop." Common Ground can take the role of tough but fair building manager, strictly enforcing rules about tenant conduct, even by eviction, while CUCS works with the tenants to help them deal with their problems so that they can maintain their residency.

Common Ground HDFC, Inc. was created by Rosanne Haggerty in order to take advantage of an opportunity to purchase the building and renovate it for its current use. Common Ground's mission is to:

> "address homelessness and joblessness through the creation of innovative programs designed to promote stability and independence for the individuals it serves while strengthening the local community."
> (from Common Ground's Strategic Plan for Year 2000)

CUCS was founded in 1981 as an organization to find placement opportunities for students from the Columbia University School of Social Work, mostly involving homeless projects. It became an independent operation in 1993, headed by Tony Hannigan.

Tony Hannigan of CUCS

The Times Square is intended as permanent — not transitional — housing. Some residents move on but that is not the focus of the program. Rather it seeks to provide good quality, supportive housing for a mixed population of low income, formerly homeless, seniors, mentally ill, or persons with AIDS. At the outset, Haggerty created a board of directors which included people with specific skills needed to launch Common Ground. The board has since expanded to increase these available skills (law, finance, etc.). In 1996 Common Ground's board completed a strategic planning process to reinforce its mission and focus on redesigning the organization for future needs.

It is a testament to Haggerty's persuasiveness and the quality of the team she assembled that this difficult project — proposed by an organization that had no track record — was able to win support from community and business leaders, and was awarded the largest SRO loan in the history of New York City.

Leadership

Common Ground, and the structure that created and operates The Times Square, emerged from the vision and energy of Rosanne Haggerty. Part of that vision, however, was in creating the structure and team that is currently in place. "She is different," said Tim O'Hanlon, of New York's Housing and Preservation Department. "She is not afraid to hire talented people. Her staff is top of the line." That also extends to CUCS staff, particularly Tony Hannigan, who is widely recognized as talented and dedicated.

When a strong individual creates a successful operation, there is always the question of how well it will survive when he or she moves on. In this case, Haggerty is already separating herself from day-to-day management, focusing most of her efforts on expanding the model to other sites. A program manager has been hired to oversee daily operations at The Times Square. Common Ground has had trouble finding experienced building managers who understood and could implement its basic philosophy. In response, it has since begun to train its own managers.

The Times Square Model

One city official suggested that The Times Square is a "poster" for an approach to dealing with homelessness and therefore many people were heavily invested in making this work — "a failure there would have been catastrophic."

The essence of The Times Square model is its use of a holistic program to maximize the independence of a needy population through the use of extensive services with a focus on economic development and the creation of jobs. Common Ground and CUCS try to adapt management and programs to the changing needs of its population instead of forcing residents to adapt to the regulations of service providers.

One of the goals of The Times Square is to show that an operation of its size can work (600+ is much larger than previously funded SROs), and in so doing use its economy of scale to provide more and better services to its population. "The biggest hurdle wasn't how to get the money to rehabilitate the building…but how to mitigate its scale."[1] Part of what they needed to overcome was the feeling of many in the field, based on experience and literature going back several decades, that large facility size in and of itself was a detriment to successful low income housing. The model attempts to mitigate the size of The Times Square in several ways:

- The plan and funding provide for **extensive social services** and staff. The facility is effectively broken down into smaller social units by providing every two floors with a four-person social service team.
- **Social services and property management are kept functionally separate**. Social services are based on a holistic "wellness" model which emphasizes helping tenants develop skills for "independent living and responsible tenancy."[1] CUCS can focus on serving resident needs, and act as a resident advocate where necessary, while Common Ground can deal with maintenance, custodial, and security issues. Social services are available for all, but are aimed at special needs tenants. Services include both on-site mental health care (counselors and psychiatrists are on staff) and health services. CUCS and Common Ground use two or three intake interviews to carefully screen applicants and eliminate people with a history of violence or who seem incapable of independent living. People with a history of substance abuse are considered only if they have been drug-free for six months and are in a treatment program.
- **A mix of special needs residents and low income, working class tenants** is meant to help "yield a stable strong community."[2] Low income but working residents, who need clean, safe affordable housing but not major social services, were included to provide a balanced population and serve as role models for others. There are many people in the theater business, for example, with low paying but steady jobs, who qualify under the provision that salary be at least three times the rent (maximum rent is $495/month). The Times Square proposal called for reserving half of the rooms for low-income working people, with the other half made up of a mix of homeless people with special needs including seniors, mentally ill, and persons with HIV/AIDS. The SRO loan from the department of Housing Preservation and Development comes with a proviso that no more than 130 units be for people earning more than 60% median income and none above 80% median income.
- **Economic development,** with a focus on businesses that provide **jobs and job training** is also an important part of The Times Square plan. Haggerty, who has been described by some as more practical than ideological, is a strong believer in the importance of economic development and job creation as one part of the solution to problems of homelessness and welfare dependency. Part of the attractiveness of The Times Square was the prime location of its ground floor retail spaces on 8th Avenue and on 43rd St. Her proposal called for attracting quality businesses, which could not only generate revenue for the operation but which would, as part of their lease, hire residents as workers. Economic development has included creating a catering business using the 15th floor facilities,

Residents and staff of The Times Square

The Ben and Jerry's Partnershop motto hangs in the store.

owning the Ben and Jerry's ice cream parlor, and rental of other retail spaces to businesses with provisions for hiring residents. With CUCS, Common Ground also provides extensive job skills training, funded by the retail rents, and in partnership with major corporations.

- Common Ground and CUCS make major efforts in **promoting jobs among tenants**. They provide training needed for jobs, including job-specific skills, resume writing, and interviewing practice, and they make available fax and phone services to help in the job search. Residents are employed by the organizations in the building (part and full time, ranging from a 4 hour a week job checking vending machines to 40+ hour administrative work), as well by outside companies. Haggerty emphasizes that there are no "make work jobs." Common Ground finds jobs for residents in part by using its good name to promise businesses that they will supply reliable and competent help.

- CUCS landed a grant from Housing and Urban Development to **provide transitional medical coverage** for workers who are leaving Medicaid but not yet included in employer health care plans.

- The **quality of the environment** in general, and **historic preservation** in particular, is another theme of this model. One of Haggerty's goals from the outset was to create a setting (in physical space and building management) that would speak of respect for the residents and set expectations for civil behavior, as demonstrated by the care and restoration that created a beautiful and dignified environment. The setting made a strong impression on one resident who, when she first walked in and saw the wide, sweeping, elegant stairway thought, "I hope they have room for me."

Haggerty sees security as critical for success. People have to feel safe living and working there. There is a security desk in the main lobby, staffed 24 hours a day, and four guards are on duty at all times. Security cameras that feed monitors at the main desk, are in the elevators and on the residential floors. In addition, all visitors must be accompanied by a resident whenever they are in the building.

The Times Square is clearly seen by New York City officials as a model for large scale SROs. The city's high regard is demonstrated not only in the SRO loan, but in its award of more than 200 hard-

The lobby of The Times Square, restored to its former elegance

The Times Square neighborhood is still in transition.

to-get Section 8 vouchers. "(Their) success made it easier for us to do this elsewhere," said Fran Reiter, former Deputy Mayor. She also noted that this project came with some risk. If it had failed it would have been hard for the city to try supportive housing of this scale again. With the strong support of the city, The Times Square model is being replicated by Common Ground at the Prince George Hotel on 28th Street.

Project Context

Times Square History — The District and the Hotel (much of this history comes from the National Register Inventory Nomination Form).

The intersection of 7th Avenue and Broadway at 42nd St. was known as Long Acre Square when it was the site of William Vanderbilt's American Horse Exchange and, in the 1890s, "silk hat" brothels serving New York's upper crust. The area obtained its current name after The New York Times opened its new building on 43rd St. between 7th and Broadway in 1904. The theater district had migrated uptown to this area by World War I. The quality of the neighborhood changed dramatically, however, with the stock market crash of 1929. As legitimate theaters closed, theater owners started showing "grinders" (continuously running, sexually explicit films). In the 1930s peep shows and prostitution increased in the area and more major theaters converted to movie houses. The trend accelerated during World War II when the district became a haven for servicemen on leave in search of prostitutes. New York City tried unsuccessfully to use zoning to reverse the trend in the 1950s. Increasingly, Times Square became home to cheap rooming houses, single room occupancy hotels, and the like. Bill Daly, head of the Mayor's Times Square Task Force, notes that in the 1970s Times Square was "a hell hole."

The history of The Times Square Hotel building reflects the growth and changes that the area itself has seen. It was erected as the Claman Hotel to cater to single men (in response to the expected arrival of returning soldiers), and "was the first hotel erected in the theater district after World War I, inaugurating a significant building boom" (National Register Inventory Nomination Form). It changed management and took the name of The Times Square Hotel in 1923, with one floor reserved for women. The hotel catered to transients, who were mostly tourists and theater goers, and permanent residents, including low wage theater workers and New York Times employees. The Times maintained several rooms for pressmen who had to work weekends. As the district changed, a series of owners reduced investment in upkeep and maintenance, making it harder to attract and keep solid, wage-earning tenants.

At one point in the 1960s it was known as The Times Square Motor Hotel. The building was in the center of an area that became rife with pornography and prostitution. In the early 1970s, The Times Square Hotel became home to the mentally ill and troubled Vietnam War veterans in large numbers and, later, the city began to place welfare recipients there. Efforts by police and case workers were overwhelmed by succeeding waves of social problems.

In 1988 the building was leased to someone who had a reputation for taking welfare payments for housing without providing support or services. The city began to use The Times Square Hotel to house homeless families, even though the rooms were inappropriate for families. Two, three or four adults and children might be crowded into rooms smaller than 300 square feet with no private bath. With children of all ages wandering the halls and reports of toddlers alone in the lobby at 3 am, The Times Square Hotel was seen as a breeding ground for drug sales, teenage prostitution, pedophilia, and crime of all sorts. Building security was virtually nonexistent and fires in rooms necessitated daily visits from the fire department. Problems from The Times Square Hotel spilled out onto the street and it became a liability in an already seedy area. 8th Ave. and 43rd St. was known at that time as the "Minnesota strip" — a center for prostitution and drugs. The Times Square Task Force created a juvenile protection unit to deal with the expanding problem of juvenile prostitution. Just when the task force felt it was starting to get a handle on some of the problems of the area, Daly said, the "crack" epidemic hit, exacerbating drug use and violence.

Common Ground

The Times Square Hotel was bought by Covenant House (known for its work with runaway children) in 1984 as a real estate investment, not with the intention of providing affordable housing. Haggerty had worked for Covenant House in 1982–83 and knew of the building, its latent charm, its tenants, its deterioration, and its possibilities. Covenant House sold it at a loss to the New York International Youth Hostel, which unsuccessfully tried to create a youth hostel there before filing for bankruptcy in 1988. When there were no bidders at auction in June of 1990, Haggerty saw an opportunity to obtain a building that could provide low income housing on a large scale. The New York City Human Resources Administration had taken over building management in 1990, and ownership reverted to the first mortgage holder, the 43rd Street Development Corporation. They had no desire to maintain or run the building and the principal, Arthur Schweibel, agreed to work with Haggerty to explore ideas for creating supportive housing in the building.

In early and mid-1990 the one other serious proposal for the building was from an established developer who had plans to divide it into two parts, each with its own entrance. Half would be a residential hotel and the other half a tourist hotel. Haggerty teamed with CUCS and worked through the summer and into the fall to create the competing proposal.

This team incorporated as Common Ground Community Housing Development Fund, Inc. and spent a great deal of time meeting with community groups, local businesses, and tenants to discuss ideas and formulate plans. On the advice of Borough President Ruth Messinger, a community advisory board was established. Haggerty obtained support and conditional approval from several key players such as The New York Times, local social service and development groups, and city officials, including then-Mayor Dinkins. Haggerty credits her quick acceptance by the city, in part, to her luck in meeting and gaining the support of Paul Crotty, well regarded former Commissioner of the City's Department of Housing and Urban Development, who became the new organization's advocate.

A number of people we interviewed noted than Haggerty had to overcome considerable initial skepticism. "I thought she was just another do-gooder," and we would have to come in and "clean up after her" said Bill Daly. He was impressed, however, when he heard her presentation with its detailed outline of services and dates for implementation ("she gave dates for moving residents and for doing renovation, and they did what they said on schedule"). Some skeptics thought that Times Square needed more business and development, and that it had more than its share of SROs. They were surprised and impressed when The New York Times and developers in the area did not object to the plan (all agree that a Times objection would have left Haggerty's proposal dead on arrival).

Haggerty won over A. O. Sulzberger, Jr., Chairman of The Times, with her clear, detailed presentation. He noted several reasons for supporting, or at least not actively opposing, her proposal. First, The Times Square Hotel was a problem for his employees, many of whom were uncomfortable walking past it on the block the two institutions share. Second, the facility was so bad that he figured she couldn't make it any worse ("As a reporter I was never in a building more horrifying. I wanted to throw up from the stench. It was a horror and I was stunned that this was fifty feet from The New York Times.") If she failed, someone else would have a chance to propose another plan. Lastly, her actions helped support the agenda of Times Square redevelopment, towards which he had been working for several years. He, and the redevelopment plan, had been criticized for concentrating on business development for the area to the exclusion of support for homeless and other disadvantaged groups. Haggerty's proposal was something he could point to in response to these criticisms.

The planning and discussions culminated at a meeting of Community Board 5. The competing developers presented their plan in what was, we were told, a rather casual manner, suggesting they had not taken the alternative plan seriously. Haggerty followed with a formal and comprehensive presentation and "had an answer for every question," said Jack Goldstein, who was the Community Board Chair at the time. All involved were impressed by the thoroughness and thoughtfulness of the plan, and the board voted overwhelmingly in support of it. One of Haggerty's and Hannigan's strengths in this process was their ability to understand and respond to the fears of local businesses. Gretchen Dykstra commented that they didn't try to make people feel guilty for not wanting panhandlers in the doorway of their stores. The strong vote for an SRO plan, she noted, was "almost unheard of. This was a heavy lift for Rosanne; she had major developers against her and she prevailed." Winning support from the Community Board was a precondition for the loan from the city's Department of Housing Preservation and Development.

Even with adequate financial resources, construction in midtown Manhattan for a new developer can be a challenge, and this project had several unique problems. Immediately after taking ownership, Common Ground and CUCS staff began to hold meetings with the elderly and mentally ill tenants, many of whom were understandably cynical about landlord promises for improvement. They had to be convinced to move twice, once for three months so their rooms could be cosmetically improved to a tolerable condition during construction, and a second time during the phased construction period. A few tenants opposed Common Ground for other reasons, convinced that a private developer would offer them "buy out" for their units. Haggerty and Hannigan concentrated on listening to tenant concerns and responding where possible with action — even small changes — that gained them a reputation for keeping promises and making repairs on time.

In addition, construction locals were upset because work was not being done with union workers at prevailing union wages. Haggerty notes that Davis-Bacon prevailing wage rules did not apply since her primary funding from New York City, as with all city SRO loans, was made based on non-union rates. She suggests that The Times Square Hotel received the brunt of the union response because of the size of the project, its geographic prominence and high visibility. The building was picketed, ambulances blocked, garbage pickup disrupted, and at one point Haggerty received bomb threats and was stalked. The action stopped when it was declared illegal by courts and the National Labor Relations Board.

Work proceeded on time in two phases. Tenants were moved from the east to the west wing while the former was renovated, and back again while work proceeded on the west wing. The building, with its renovated units in the east wing, was opened 14 months after construction began, in February, 1993. In addition to the original residents, almost 200 new tenants moved in. Common Ground and CUCS ran a series of meetings to help the two groups integrate smoothly. The remaining units were opened 14 months later. Common Ground and CUCS phased in their full staff, working continuously with old and new tenants through this long

The Times Square lobby features a grand marble staircase.

13

phase-in process to bring the building on-line with a minimum of problems.

Current Status and Impact

On entering the lobby the casual visitor has few if any reminders of the mixed, and in some cases difficult population being housed there. Much of the former elegance of the building has been restored, and the facility appears to be well maintained by Common Ground staff and the tenants (see "Design and Maintenance").

The Times Square's facility operating expenses are covered by rent (including Section 8 subsidies) and the considerable social service efforts are paid for by contracts with city and state social service agencies (mostly through the Department of Mental Health). Profits from retail operations fund the job training programs. 1700 square feet of additional retail space has been renovated and is available for rent (see "financing").

The facility is full and annual turnover is low — about 16%. Most turnover consists of people who seek bigger apartments, who marry, or who take jobs in other places. The eviction rate is less than 1%. Haggerty estimates that about 5 to 10 residents leave annually for other reasons. Some "bolt" when confronted with nonpayment of rent, and others leave for more structured settings. She also notes that the death rate of tenants is down considerably (about 7 per year at first), largely due to improved medication for the treatment of AIDS.

Common Ground and The Times Square have had a positive impact in three areas — on the lives of residents, on the neighborhood, and on city policy. The original residents are living in far better and safer physical and social conditions and under more watchful care than previously. For new residents it provides safe, affordable housing and an opportunity to live independently and develop improved living skills. Seventy-three residents work for CUCS or Common Ground-owned and run operations (including Ben and Jerry's), and 80 residents have been placed in outside jobs (including Starbucks) since November, 1995. The average salary for these jobs is $18,500 per year.

An actor and resident of The Times Square is pleased with his home.

SROs are usually seen as being a drawback in a neighborhood, but this one has provided a needed lift. While all of the district is improving now — due to massive city efforts and the influx of substantial development dollars — when The Times Square renovation began in 1991, plans to upgrade the area were in disarray. The Times Square was one of the first successes in the area. Not only has it created a safer and more comfortable feel to that part of 43rd Street, it has become an active partner with The Times Square Business Improvement District and others working to improve the area.

Prior to The Times Square, no facilities of this size had been considered for SRO loans or other support. In addition to having supported The Times Square, the current city administration is actively supporting Common Ground's next development project. The Times Square has had other policy impacts, as well. For example, they struggled at first to get approval for funding for housing support for their AIDS patients from the Division of AIDS Services, which had previously funded people in institutional settings. Now this agency regularly funds supportive housing settings.

The 43rd Street entrance to The Times Square

Design and Maintenance

"The Times Square is a Renaissance-inspired fifteen story tan-colored brick building with a two story white limestone base and limestone-colored terra-cotta trim. The 43rd Street elevation is divided into four wings, separated by light courts, and connected by the two-story rusticated limestone base."[3] One enters through a bronze revolving door and into a vestibule with a terrazzo floor and ornate plaster ceiling. The interior L-shaped lobby has "pink marble walls set on a black marble base, brown terrazzo floor with red and black terrazzo details, and ornate plaster ceiling." The lobby is two-stories high "with a cast-iron mezzanine balcony lined with a Neoclassic railing…supported on square marble piers," reached by prominent, curving stairways with bronze railings.

There were several design challenges in renovating The Times Square to serve as supportive housing. Common Ground had to find a way to renovate the building while 30% of the rooms were occupied, reconfigure the floor plan so that all rooms had baths and most had kitchenettes, plan space for social service offices and program rooms, and do all this within the context of restoring and maintaining the historic character of the building. The reconstruction reduced the number of units from 735 to 652, mostly because of expanded room size for the baths.

Rooms range in size from 250 to 350 square feet and resemble the long narrow configuration of college dormitory rooms. While none could be called spacious, they comfortably accommodate single occupants. Eighty percent of the apartments have kitchenettes, a small bed (with a storage drawer underneath), a bath, cable TV and closets or armoires. The typical residential floor is served by three passenger elevators with 50 units on a double loaded corridor. Each floor has central space set aside as a community activity room (used for painting, computers, crafts, etc.). Haggerty disliked the rapid deterioration of carpet in other buildings she had seen, so high quality, polished vinyl composition tiles were used in hallways. Metropolitan Life's facility manager volunteered many hours testing waxes to find the best combination for maintenance.

Elise Quasebarth, the preservation consultant to Common Ground, was impressed that Haggerty saw the importance of the historic character of the building, and was committed to its preservation, given that the building was not a New York City landmark, and therefore not subject to design control regulations.

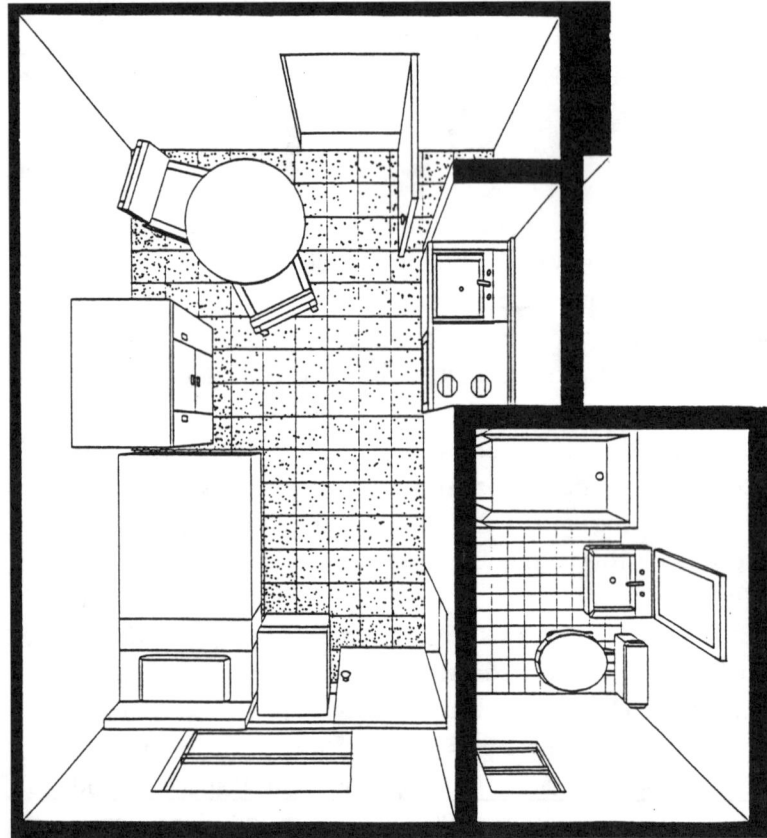

Plan of a typical room at the Times Square

While Haggerty was always attracted to the architectural character of the building, the level and quality of the restoration and preservation details came to the fore in April 1992 when they decided to apply for historic preservation tax credits, requiring that work be done to U.S. Department of Interior standards.

One of the most difficult arguments came when Common Ground's plan to put private baths in every room was challenged as a significant variation from the original configuration. Private baths were a critical element of the functional plan for the building's operation, however, and Common Ground fought hard and won on this point. Common Ground also won permission to extend the mezzanine walkway around the entire second floor, allowing easy access among all offices. Some restoration features were quite expensive, such as the more than $100,000 spent on restoring the special multi-pane casement windows in the mezzanine and second floor.

There was also significant opposition to the construction of catering and dining facilities on the roof, creating a 15th floor. The addition was eventually approved when it was determined that it was not easily visible from most views of the building.

Common Ground and CUCS offices are on the mezzanine floor. CUCS staff have ample office space which is arranged so that teams are together. The basement is currently undergoing a renovation that will add considerable program space. It will include several classrooms, an employee out placement center, a computer center with several dozen donated machines, a music rehearsal space, a photography club dark room, and food pantry storage. They have also leased basement space to a florist for storage.

Residents say that Common Ground is very responsive to their problems and complaints. Most are extremely positive about the facility, and say that it is "heaven" in comparison to most alternatives. Their only significant design complaint is the lack of closet space, something Common Ground has noted and addressed in its next project. Common Ground recognizes that the upkeep of the facility is critical to its operation and quality of life, and expends considerable funds and energy in maintenance and cleaning, and also in supporting residents to take care of their own apartments.

On the street level there are several thousand square feet of retail space. Starbucks and Ben and Jerry's franchises occupy the 8th Avenue side. Common Ground owns the ice cream franchise, which was given to them as part of Ben and Jerry's corporate "partner-shop" program. 1700 square feet of space on 43rd St. is still unoccupied. Common Ground is a choosy landlord which has turned down many offers, preferring to wait for a "quality" business that can hire and train residents and be a stabilizing force on the block.

Financing

Common Ground was fortunate in having access to a variety of sources that effectively over-funded acquisition and construction, leaving significant capital to support new initiatives and act as a buffer for any future funding cuts. Operating expenses for the building are covered by rents. The $1.7 million social service budget, through CUCS, is funded through contracts with the Department of Mental Health, the SRO Support Services Program, and the Division of AIDS Services. This gives the operators of The Times Square the ability to provide a high quantity and quality of social services and facility maintenance. It reduces the risk of sudden demise due to the failure of an annual campaign or catastrophic cuts in social funding, assuring continuity of operations and freeing them to focus on new programs or projects.

The acquisition and construction costs (approximately $36 million) were covered mainly by the largest ever New York City loan for development of permanent SRO housing. The city provided almost $29 million for 30 years, at 1% interest. This loan required Common Ground to apply for Low Income Housing Tax

Operating Budget

Income

Rental Income (assumes 2% vac. & 10% uncollectable)	$3,080,000
DAS support	$128,920
Other income (vending, cable, storage, etc.)	$221,110
Total Income	**$3,430,030**

Expenses

Personnel (payroll & benefits)	$1,437,492
Security (contracts, fire alarms, etc.)	$197,500
Maintenance (housekeeping, maintenance, landscaping, painting, etc.)	$151,160
Utilities (gas, electric, water, etc.)	$501,450
General & Administration (supplies, phone, copier, etc.)	$75,324
Tenant Services (vending, special programs, meal subsidies)	$83,700
Professional & Consulting Services (legal, audit, insurance)	$240,060
Fees (management fee, debt service, reserve, etc.)	$672,942
Total Expenses	**$3,359,628**
Capital Expenditures (phone leases, equip., contingency)	$66,388
Surplus	$4,014

Major corporations such as Starbucks and Ben & Jerry's provide job training opportunities for tenants.

Development Costs

Uses

Acquisition	$9,533,949
Construction	$16,149,000
Contingency	$2,460,881
Furnishings	$816,000
Architect	$997,990
Fees, insurance, etc.	$1,066,299
Taxes	$1,046,248
Bridge Loan Interest	$749,968
Sub-total	*$32,820,335*
Working Capital	$2,126,084
Developer's Fee	$1,173,600
Total Acq./Construct.	**$36,120,019**

Capitalized Reserve

Operating reserve	$9,079,839
Sponsor operating reserve	$2,973,456
Social service reserve	$2,973,456
Sub-total	*$15,026,751*
Total Uses	**$51,146,770**

Sources

NYC HPD SRO Loan Program	$28,850,108
Tax Credit Equity & Met. Life Bridge Loan	$22,156,662
Time Square Public	$140,000
Total Sources	**$51,146,770**

Credits and later Common Ground also applied for Historic Rehabilitation Tax Credits which, when syndicated and sold at $.80 to the dollar yielded over $22 million of additional capital, providing much of the surplus noted above. The preservation credits resulted in some additional expenses, but most of the preservation requirements were already in the plan.

Rent and profits from retail tenants currently yield about $100,000 per year. These funds are used exclusively for job training programs. "Robin Hood" rates are used for commercial tenants, with rental charges reflecting, in part, the number of resident jobs provided.

Metropolitan Life Foundation provided a bridge loan of $2.5 million which allowed construction of the 15th floor addition, including the kitchen and common space for residents. Street level retail space was renovated with the support of a New York State Urban Development Corporation grant of $234,050. Many other foundations (Bankers Trust, Newman's Own, Robin Hood, Altman, Tiger, John Merck, Rhodebeck) have provided substantial loans and grants to support economic development programs.

Common Ground maintains that this housing, under $11,000 per person per year, including all social service programs, is cost effective in that it is significantly less than the cost of supporting someone in a homeless shelter, psychiatric hospital or prison.

Current Projects and Future Plans

Common Ground's current major project is the renovation of the Prince George Hotel, on 28th Street, with 416 rooms of supportive housing. The Prince George Hotel is based on The Times Square model. In the face of some initial opposition to this plan from some local groups and corporations, Common Ground received testimonials and support from its Times Square neighbors and the city. David Klasfeld, of the Deputy Mayor's Office, effectively told organizations in the Prince George Hotel area that the city fully supported the project and that they could call his office at any time to discuss any problems that might arise.

Common Ground's recent strategic plan calls for further expansion and directs staff to purchase a third large hotel for supportive housing. It also proposes developing several smaller scale projects for people not capable of independent living in supportive housing. The strategic plan emphasizes the need for continued economic development, calling for an increase of job production, as well as business and training programs to provide better work experiences for residents. It suggests Common Ground seek out and identify new economic development and training models in partnership with businesses and entrepreneurs. The plan also notes the need to expand Common Ground's organizational infrastructure to meet the needs of an expanded operation. Working with local community groups and sharing services with other supportive housing organizations could increase services at less cost.

Assessing Project Success

How Well The Times Square is Meeting its Goals

- *To restore a historic hotel without displacing residents.*
  The restoration was completed without displacing residents, met high standards of historic preservation, and provides a high quality, functional setting for residents, staff and programs.
- *To "address homelessness and joblessness through the creation of innovative programs designed to promote stability and independence."*
  Common Ground has had significant success in providing opportunities for job training and placement in real jobs within the organization, in businesses located in the street level shops, and in jobs outside the building.
- *Provide decent, permanent housing for low income adults, people with mental and physical disabilities, or AIDS.*
  A wide mix of people with mental and physical disabilities live harmoniously with low income adults. Support services are sufficient to make it possible for all residents to live independently.

Starbucks occupies a prime location on 43rd Street.

- *To convert a building that was a "trouble spot" on an already difficult block to one that supports and promotes the renewal of Times Square.*
  The Times Square has become a positive force, socially and physically, in the regeneration of Times Square, and is recognized as such by many who were initial opponents to the creation of supportive housing at that site.
- *To provide a model for successful, large-scale single room occupancy hotels in an urban context.*
  The Times Square has become a model for large scale SRO development and operations. It is being copied by Common Ground itself in other developments, and is mentioned as a model by city agencies and observers from other cities.

Response to Selection Committee Questions and Concerns

- *What is the population in the building and how does it work? Do people get along or are there conflicts and antagonisms?*
The population is very mixed (elderly, low income, mentally ill, HIV/AIDS), but seems to get along well, thanks to a large and attentive staff, and a strong set of social, health, and job-related programs. Problems are identified and dealt with quickly, and residents are aware of rules and expectations for behavior.

- *What sort of changes do people living in the building experience in their own life cycles (e.g., how many move "up" and out to permanent housing; how many drift back to the streets)?*
This **is** permanent housing, so for many, especially the mentally ill, this is where they want to be. Some others are moving out as they find jobs that pay well or are in other cities, or as they decide they need more space. Few seem to "drop out back to the street," and eviction rates are low. The operation seems to be very successful at finding ways for this high risk population to achieve independence through supported living.

- *What are the social services offered in the building, to what level are they utilized (number of residents, content, quality, contact hours)? Are services adequate? How are they funded and how stable is the funding (is it endowed or capitalized)?*
Social services are heavily utilized and include mental health and medical services, counseling, job training and placement. Services are funded by government programs and funds from retail operations, with the capital reserve as backup.

- *What was the design process? Were the residents involved in the design? Was anyone involved who was sensitive to or knowledgeable about this group's needs?*
The facility design was developed from the experience of Common Ground and CUCS staff, in consultation with preservationists, and through discussions with community leaders and residents of the building. The staff involved in this project has a great deal of experience with this population and appears very sensitive to their needs.

- *What is the quality of the design and materials?*
Design and materials are generally of high quality and well done, with considerable sensitivity to preservation issues and to tenant needs. Insufficient storage is the one common complaint among tenants. The sense of community and quality of the social environment is evidence of the effectiveness of the staff interventions, given that long, double-loaded corridors in a high density building do not naturally lend themselves to a positive social atmosphere.

- *Has any follow-up been done on how the design is working? Or on resident satisfaction with it?*
Meetings, discussions, focus groups and "gripe sessions" with residents have yielded comments, but there have been no formal post occupancy studies. Based on resident comments, some changes have been made at The Times Square, and modifications to the design, such as increasing closet space, are planned for Prince George.

- *What is the organization for managing the building? Is there self-management; are residents involved? Are maintenance activities and budgets adequate?*
Common Ground manages the building and is very attentive to custodial and security matters. Maintenance is well funded. Residents are involved through tenant-management association meetings (although it is not clear how much real input these associations have). Many tenants have been hired to do jobs in the building.

- *How do neighbors view the project (shop owners, property owners and developers)?*
Neighbors with whom we spoke are very positive. The New York

Times, sees it as a major asset to the neighborhood; the manager of a nearby new luxury hotel thinks The Times Square has helped improve the neighborhood; and the owner of a local "mom and pop" store sees the facility as innocuous (in this case being largely invisible is a positive indicator for an SRO). Local community groups are thrilled with their work and support Common Ground in other community efforts.

- *Does the project have any relationship to the major renewal of the Times Square neighborhood?*
  Yes. It was one of the first successes in the area, and is one of the few social service projects that is part of the redevelopment. The facility houses sanitation staff who work for The Times Square Business Improvement District (BID), and is involved in many BID efforts. Residents have taken jobs with local businesses, and low income workers in the area have applied for residence.

Impact on the Neighborhood

The Times Square has helped improve the quality of life on 8th Avenue and 43rd Street, in an area with one of the worst reputations in New York City. Its management shows concern for the area and for activity on its sidewalk, helping discourage panhandling and antisocial behaviors on the block. It has gone from being a negative force — a detriment to the block and a place working people were uncomfortable walking past — to a positive force. It provides inexpensive housing for local low income laborers and works closely with the BID and other local organizations with whom Common Ground has many overlapping board members. Common Ground is also using its expertise to help other supportive housing projects in the area, and has contracted to manage another facility.

Quality of the Physical Place

Common Ground was committed to completing a serious restoration of the building even before historic restoration tax credits came into play. The building is attractive and very well maintained, and appears to be treated well by both staff and tenants. The Times Square provides a safe, excellent environment for its residents and tenant businesses.

Values

The Times Square embodies Common Ground's core values which are to provide "innovative and cost effective ways of addressing homelessness and joblessness," and to create "strong, supportive communities" that are capable of helping implement programs. Common Ground places a strong emphasis on the use of economic development to provide jobs for its residents, as a tool to improve the clients' lives, and to increase their capacity for independence.

Leadership

Rosanne Haggerty, with the considerable aid and support of Tony Hannigan, provided most of the vision and tenacity required to get this project off the ground. This was a high-risk effort and not easy to sell to the community. Haggerty is now working to develop increased capacity within the organization so that it can sustain itself, and has separated herself from daily management.

Sustainability

In spite of the strong role Haggerty and Hannigan had in creating the program, the operation does not appear dependent on any one or two individuals. The bifurcated structure, separating building management from social services, allows staff to concentrate on a limited range of specific tasks, while working together to view the bigger picture when necessary. Its funding structure and the significant reserve fund make The Times Square unusually financially stable.

This does not mean that there are no risks for the future of The Times Square. In a building of this size, with this population, the level of programs and staffing needs to remain high. A major and prolonged cut of government programs, like Section 8 vouchers, for example, could deplete their reserve fund.

Selection Committee Comments

The Selection Committee, in awarding The Times Square the 1997 Rudy Bruner Award Gold Medal, expressed great admiration for Common Ground's ability to make this project work on a number of levels. They were appreciative of the way the building was restored, and the care and attention that were given to preservation detail while remaining an SRO. The quality of the lobby restoration, for example, was seen as evidence of respect for the dignity of The Times Square tenants.

The Selection Committee felt that using an entrepreneurial approach to "create an effective instrument" to address the serious unmet need of this population was a remarkable accomplishment, particularly at this scale. The Times Square has had a positive impact on peoples lives and on an important city block.

The Committee did not find any serious flaws in this project. It felt that the Times Square provides a model for other facilities and other cities, in terms of the scale of the project, the mix of population and services involved. They also were impressed by the way its goals were accomplished in a cost-effective and financially sustainable fashion.

Endnotes

1. Taken from Common Ground's Application to the 1997 Rudy Bruner Award
2. Blake, Jennifer, "*The Times Square: A Case Study of Supportive Housing,*" Metropolitan Life Foundation
3. National Register Inventory Nomination Form, Part 7: Description

References

Blake, Jennifer. "*The Times Square: A Case Study in Supportive Housing,*" The Development Training Institute, Inc.: Baltimore, Md., 1996.

Common Ground Community HDFC, Inc. *Strategic Plan for the Year 2000*, 1996.

National Register Inventory Nomination Form, "The Times Square" submitted by Andrew S. Dolkart, January, 1993.

For more information

Common Ground Community HDFC, Inc.
255 West 43rd Street
New York, NY 10036

TEL: 212-768-8989

WEB SITE: www.commonground.org

silver MEDAL 1997

Project Row Houses
Houston, Texas

Project Row Houses (PRH) at a Glance

What Is Project Row Houses?

- 22 historic "shotgun" style houses which were previously abandoned and have been transformed into a complex of art gallery/installation space, and social programs.
- An urban revitalization program which includes 8 houses for art installations; 7 houses for young, single mothers; a center for mixed media and performing arts, a day care and after-school program, a center for empowerment programs for African-American women, and a community garden.
- A national model which is being adapted to other inner-city locations. The hallmarks of the model are the combined use of local historic structures, art forms growing out of community cultural identity, and social programs responsive to local community needs.

Who Made the Submission?

- Project Row Houses, a nonprofit organization which owns and operates the project.

Major Goals of PRH

- To restore an historic site in Houston's inner city;
- To create a center for visual, written, and performing art which showcases the work of African-American artists, while creating a strong connection between the community and its African-American heritage;
- To create opportunity in Houston's Third Ward by modeling African-American artistic achievement in combination with social programs geared toward educational opportunity and self-reliance;
- To establish a model for reclamation of inner-city neighborhoods with art as catalyst to stimulate constructive dialogue addressing cultural, educational, economic, and social issues.

Major Accomplishments of PRH

- Rehabilitation of historic "shotgun" houses for art, housing, day care and after-school programs;
- Creation of an art program in 8 Gallery Houses, where prominent African-American artists utilize row houses for art installation and community workshops;
- Development of the Young Mothers Residential Program (YMRP) which provides transitional housing and life-skills training for young single mothers between the ages of 17 and 24;

Project Row Houses announces its opening.

- Acquisition of a contiguous 2 story building which PRH intends to rehabilitate for performing arts, offices, and community gatherings;
- Participation in projects in four other cities utilizing the PRH model for community revitalization.

Reasons for Including PRH as a finalist

- The focus on art as a tool to model cultural achievement and engage the community in interactive workshops;
- The potential for achieving multiple goals—providing transitional housing, stabilizing lives, combining art with social programs; offering a brighter future to community residents;
- Use of culturally significant historic houses for quality housing, gallery space, and social programs, in an art-based context.

Selection Committee Questions and Concerns for Site Visit

- Does PRH change the community/neighborhood vision of itself?
- Does the Third Ward now feel like a special place?
- Is PRH a real, active place, not just a group of historic structures?
- How has PRH affected the Houston business community?
- Who walks down the street? What is the feeling of the neighborhood?
- How real are they? Is this one person's vision, or is there an organization growing here?
- Is the project financially stable?
- Is the project connected to a network of support in the community? In city government? In the business community?
- What are the spin-offs and current and future plans? Where are they going next? What are they doing in Watts and East St. Louis?

Final Selection Committee Comments

- PRH was recognized as an innovative project, making an important statement about the place of art in community revitalization and its ability to make connections across traditional barriers.
- PRH is a grass-roots organization, operating outside the accepted channels of government, and demonstrating a degree of flexibility which enabled to respond to community needs. This suggests an innovative model which may well be outside of traditional funding patterns or boundaries.
- While PRH was commended for its originality, the Committee felt it was too early to judge its lasting impact.

Project Description

Chronology

1990–1992 A group of African-American artists, including Rick Lowe, begin to meet periodically to discuss ways of enriching their community through the development of temporary public art installations in African-American neighborhoods.

Summer, 1992 Rick Lowe discovers 22 abandoned identical "shotgun"-style houses in Houston's Third Ward. The site seems ideal for the installation of art works due to the cultural significance of these houses, their significance in African-American history, and their location. Initial contact is made with owner.

Spring, 1993 PRH was awarded $6,000 from the Cultural Arts Council of Houston, and $25,000 from the National Endowment for the Arts (NEA) for preservation of the houses, and launching of the arts program. NEA shows PRH slides to the National Council and holds it up as a model community arts project. Houston's Housing and Community Development

Department agrees that PRH will be considered for a 1994–95 Community Development Block Grant budget.

September, 1993 Five year lease/purchase of 22 row houses negotiated with owner, for $100,000 at $1,000/month. Artists lead community volunteers to clear site of trash and weeds.

October, 1993 Deborah Grotfeldt, formerly with DiverseWorks Art Space, joins PRH as Managing Director to develop and organize programs, develop budgets, implement fund-raising and write grant proposals.

March, 1994 Founding Board of Directors meeting and elect officers. Heimbinder Family Foundation loans PRH $126,000 for outright purchase of property, and accepts burden of $26,000 in back property taxes.

May–June 1994 Amoco/Home Depot and their employees contribute materials and volunteer labor to complete exterior renovation of 12 houses.

October, 1994 Inaugural installations open with works by eight prominent Texas African-American artists. Over 1,000 people attend.

April, 1995 The Meadows Foundation in Dallas grants $100,000 to the Young Mothers Residential Program (YMRP).

June, 1995 YMRP mentor family moves in. Work begins on rehabilitation of YMRP houses with support from MASCO Corporation, Women's Day Special Interest Publications, and U.S. Home Corp.

February, 1996 Five families headed by single mothers move into YMRP houses.

June, 1996 $50,000 grant to support artists' installations received from Rockefeller Foundation.

December, 1996 Funds to buy adjacent parcel loaned to PRH by Heimbinder Foundation; land cost is reduced by half by owner.

Key Participants *(persons interviewed are indicated by an asterisk*)*

Project Row Houses
  Rick Lowe, *Founding Director**
  Deborah Grotfeldt, *Executive Director**
  James England, *President of the Board* (*phone)
  Dr. Nelda Lewis, *Young Mother's Residential Program* (*phone)

Heimbinder Family Foundation
  Isaac Heimbinder, *Board* (*phone)
  Sheila Heimbinder, *Board, YMRP Coordinator* (*phone)

University of Houston, Department of Architecture
  Sheryl G. Tucker, *Architect**

Rice University School of Architecture
  Nanya Grenada, *Architect**

Cultural Arts Council of Houston and Harris County
  Jessica Cussick, *Public Arts and Urban Design Director*

Houston City Council
  Councilman Jew Don Boney*

Houston Department of Community Development
  Ken Bolton, *Asst. Director**
  Tom Doyle, *Community Planner**
  S. Teffera, *Statistician**

Amoco Corporation
  Cory S. Webster, *Executive Director, Amoco Torch Classic**

The Vision

Project Row Houses is the personal vision of founder Rick Lowe. As a young artist influenced by the work of his teacher, prominent African-American artist John Biggers, and by a growing feeling of alienation from the mainstream art world, Lowe began seeking ways to reconnect African-American art and artists with the community. Based upon his work with Biggers, who had also researched "shotgun" houses and used them as an important element in his painting, Lowe developed the belief that art had the potential to transform the community in several important ways: by creating positive cultural images of African-American identity; by showcasing the artistic accomplishments of African-American artists; by bringing people from all economic and social levels into the community; and by engaging them in a meaningful dialogue about the issues raised by the art itself. This notion of the transformative power of art has been the driving force behind Project Row Houses (PRH), and while PRH has grown beyond this initial concept to include other programs, Lowe's vision remains crucial to the identity of the project.

Project Row Houses and the Third Ward

The selection of the PRH site was both deliberate and fortuitous. Although not a Houston native, Rick Lowe had developed connections in the Third Ward through his association with SHAPE Community Center. Lowe hoped to establish an African-American art installation there because of his connection with the community and because revitalization was desperately needed in that area. In the shadow of downtown Houston, the demographic profile of the Third Ward is typical of the nation's inner city neighborhoods. The Third Ward is 98% African-American, and is characterized by extreme poverty, with 40% of household incomes under $5,000. There is a large amount of vacant or abandoned property, with a 40% land use vacancy rate for the area. Education levels are low. 59% of those under the age of 25 never completed high school, and over half of the children in the Third Ward are born to single teen mothers and raised below the poverty level.

Despite its bleak demographic profile, however, the Third Ward has some important assets. It has not yet seen systematic demolition of dilapidated housing to make way for denser more costly development, as has occurred in other Houston neighborhoods.

Rick Lowe, Founder

A front porch in The Third Ward neighborhood

In addition, the Third Ward has some powerful neighbors including University of Houston, Texas Southern University, the Museum of fine Arts and Texas Medical Center, located at the boundaries of the district. While the proximity of these major institutions raises the specter of future encroachment into the neighborhood, the Third Ward's MacGregor neighborhood, filled with large, landscaped, and attractive single family homes, has remained in good condition, and is now occupied by upper middle class African-Americans, who have contributed to stabilization of the community.

From Vision to Reality

When Rick Lowe stumbled upon the abandoned "shotgun" houses, he felt strongly that the Third Ward location, the importance of "shotgun" houses to African-American history, and the nature, quality and configuration of the buildings made it an ideal location for the art initiative he envisioned. Lowe worked for a year to locate the owner in order to lease 10 "shotgun" houses for a temporary public art installation. The owner, however, insisted that all 22 houses be included in the transaction. By that time, Lowe, Grotfeldt, and others involved felt that the project could use the additional houses for programs which related to other community concerns and interests.

The negotiation of the lease/purchase agreement marked an important turning point for PRH. Soon after that Deborah Grotfeldt came to PRH from DiverseWorks Arts Space where she had served as Assistant Director. She helped to obtain critical nonprofit status, established the legal, financial and administrative systems which are in place today, and began major fund-raising efforts. Together, Lowe and Grotfeldt worked at project financing, developing relationships in the community, planning programs, and recruiting and managing volunteers and contractors who performed the initial site clearance, clean-up and rehabilitation.

Between the Fall of 1993 and the Spring of 1994, PRH established itself as a nonprofit entity, recruited an influential board of directors which included prominent professionals from the legal profession, major art institutions, and the housing industry. It enlisted the support of a significant volunteer base through Amoco Corporation and the art community. Although it was a productive period, it was not without its difficulties. Despite its ostensible support for PRH, in September of 1993 the City of Houston identified the houses as "dangerous buildings," and threatened to demolish them. Although this status was later revoked, trust between the City and the project was damaged.

This period of intense organization culminated in June 1994, with the restoration of the exterior of 12 houses through volunteer help and materials from Amoco and Home Depot. This was the first of many major volunteer efforts and was the beginning of a series of important milestone events. Later that summer the "House Challenge" resulted in the completion of eight Gallery

A Third Ward Street adjacent to Project Row Houses.

Houses, each of which was sponsored by established players in the Houston Arts community, including the Museum of fine Arts, the Menil Collection, the Museum of Contemporary Art, DiverseWorks, a neighborhood church, and an African-American sorority. Their names hang on the transom of each gallery.

While lease payments had been made on the site through a series of grants, it was not until March 1994, that PRH finally acquired all 22 houses through a loan from the Heimbinder Family Foundation. In April 1995 the Meadows Foundation gave $100,000 to the Young Mothers Residential Program, ensuring that the program would move ahead. Near the same time, in June 1995, US Home, and its President, Isaac Heimbinder, entered into a collaboration with MASCO Corporation and Women's Day Special Interest Publications to design, renovate and furnish houses for residences and a day care center for the Young Mother's Program. This collaboration resulted in seven houses being decorated and furnished by different Houston interior designers. The results were published in a national magazine, showcasing the attractive and distinctly different furnished houses. The YMRP program was then launched, and five young, single teen mothers and their children, along with a mentor, moved into the houses.

The momentum and energy which characterizes PRH has continued to grow. PRH now includes a variety of programs, housed in the 22 row houses. While the Gallery Houses, the daily after-school program, and the Young Mothers Residential Program are the cornerstones of the PRH social programs, PRH has remained flexible and demonstrated an ability to implement programs which are responsive to the needs of the Third Ward. Today PRH includes not only a day care program and an after-school program, but also Spoken Word House, a variety of empowerment programs run for African-American women, and a community garden.

The relationship between PRH and the Third Ward community appears strong. The community benefits directly from the PRH programs, and PRH has contributed to a sense of pride in community as increasing numbers of visitors come into the neighborhood. It is notable that PRH galleries and offices are open all day, yet there has not yet been a single incident of theft or vandalism. According to Rev. Robert McGee, the Pastor of Trinity United Methodist Church, the project is "like a blood transfusion; it has given life to the community."

The Architecture

The row houses are architecturally significant buildings, and their preservation and restoration has engendered support from the larger architectural community and two major universities, as well as from the neighborhood. The history of the row house, from West Africa to Haiti and the southern United States has been studied both by African-American artists such as John Biggers, and architectural historians. The historic "shotgun" house consists of two rooms of similar size, one in the front of the house and one in the back. The term "shotgun" is associated with the fact that the front and back doors are aligned, thus making it possible for a gun shot to pass through the house without hitting anything inside. In February 1994 the Texas Historical Commission determined that the PRH houses were eligible for inclusion in the National Register of Historic Places. PRH received one of only 16 Honor Awards from the National Trust for Historic preservation in the fall of 1997.

The row houses are striking in their simplicity. Approaching PRH from Holman Street, one sees two blocks of identical one story row house facades, each painted white, with corrugated tin roofs overlaid with a brown patina of rust and age. There is a distinct visual rhythm inherent in the repetition of these simple forms. Many of the houses have modest plantings in front of them, but for the most part the appearance is plain, almost stark. Behind Holman

Project Row Houses facades after rehabilitation

Street, a second row of houses is located directly opposite, creating a small interior avenue of open space. This space, where back porches face each other, creates a communal area, where children play in the after-school and day-care programs, and where neighbors have a natural awareness of each others' comings and goings (see photos). In the future, the performing arts center planned at the terminus of the gallery houses will form a visual and functional edge to this communal "back yard."

African-American artist John Biggers, who has incorporated the row houses as a theme in his work makes the following statement about similar houses in the adjacent Fourth Ward: "I see them as I walk the Fourth Ward of Houston, the rhythm of their light and shadow, the triangle of their gables, the square of the porch, three over four, like the beat of a visual gospel."

PRH has been fortunate in its connection with architects who understand and are committed to the PRH vision. In November of 1993, in response to a grant request to HUD, PRH joined forces with Sheryl Tucker, an architect who developed a master plan for PRH as part of her design studio at the University of Houston School of Architecture. Ms. Tucker became actively interested in PRH and in the conservation of the "shotgun" houses, and applied for and received a grant of $25,000 from the National Endowment for the Arts to develop a site master plan and architectural documents for the row houses. These drawings were displayed at the initial opening of PRH and formed the basis for the volunteer rehabilitation work.

In Sheryl Tucker's view, "the project has also helped many people understand that the "shotgun" house, the predominant housing type of the community, is not a symbol of shame associated with slavery, but a concrete visual link to African housing traditions as documented by architectural historians." Their restoration symbolizes a departure from the culture of neglect that has long characterized the area. Ms. Tucker remains architectural consultant and Board member for PRH, and is currently involved in developing a design for the new two story building to be restored on the recently acquired corner property.

A second architectural resource for PRH is the Rice Building Workshop led by Nanya Grenada, professor of Architecture at Rice University. The workshop will focus on the design and construction of a new prototype row house, to occupy the vacant land recently purchased behind the Young Mothers houses.

The maintenance of the houses is supported by volunteer efforts of Chevron and Amoco, both of whom periodically volunteer at PRH. The houses are attractive and well-maintained, and during our visit the Amoco team toured the site to discuss the maintenance needs for an upcoming volunteer day.

Financing Project Row Houses

Project Row Houses has been financed by a series of grants from arts agencies, foundations and corporations. The acquisition of the row houses through a loan from the Heimbinder Foundation, and a major grant from the Meadows Foundation for the Young Mothers Program, enabled PRH to establish direction and to secure a series of grants and loans from a variety of private and public entities. While these grants have met the financial needs of the project to date, the limitations of grant-based funding have also limited the scope of PRH's operations and expansion. PRH remains dependent upon the short term funding horizon associated with renewal of grants and the ongoing quest for additional funding sources.

While PRH is limited by its short funding horizon, it continues to secure the funds required to run the programs currently in place and to support new initiatives. While the Board has encouraged planning for additional programs and initiatives, they have also been careful to ensure that PRH runs existing programs successfully and within the means available to it. The Board is proud of the positive impact PRH has had on the community.

Interior courtyard at Project Row Houses before renovation.

Interior courtyard after renovation. Back doors face each other in a communal back yard.

Projected Budget:
September 1, 1996–August 31, 1997

Revenues

Beginning Balance	$99,159
Government Grants *(subtotal)*	$68,086
NEA (pending)	$10,000
TCA (committed)	$13,042
CACHH (committed)	$45,044
Corporations	$45,000
Foundations	$110,000
Fund Raising Events	$55,000
Total Revenues	**$377,245**

Expenses

Operations *(subtotal)*	$213,145
Mortgage	$8,540
Salaries	$118,550
Payroll Taxes	$11,855
Benefits	$15,000
Contract	$13,200
Utilities	$5,400
Telephone	$5,000
Office Supplies	$4,000
Office Expense	$4,000
Office Equipment	$1,000
Postage	$1,800
Liability Insurance	$2,000
Auto Insurance	$3,300
Auto Expense	$5,000
Site Maintenance	$3,000
Documentation	$1,500
Miscellaneous	$10,000
Art and Cultural Education *(subtotal)*	$108,000
Artist Installations	$68,000
After School/Summer	$40,000
Young Mothers Residential Program	$13,600
Planning	$10,000
Total Expenses	**$344,745**

Isaac Heimbinder was optimistic that as PRH becomes better known, and demonstrates its ability to run quality programs, it will become easier to attract funds.

Despite some conflicting messages from representatives of city government (see below), it seems possible that PRH will ultimately receive some additional funding from the City of Houston. The City Council is well aware of PRH, and the project is gaining sufficient visibility to improve its prospects of receiving additional public funds. Given PRH's plans for the future, City assistance in future property acquisition and expansion will be critical.

Project Row Houses and the City of Houston

The relationship between Project Row Houses and the City of Houston has been complicated. On the positive side, as early as the Spring of 1993, PRH was meeting with the Housing and Community Development Department to explore the possibilities for City funding. Initially the Department was supportive, indicating that PRH would be eligible for 1994–95 Community Development Block Grant funds. At about the same time, PRH was awarded $6,000 from the Cultural Arts Council of Houston, one of the first grants awarded to the project.

By the Fall of 1993, both the City Council and the mayor were vocal supporters of PRH. In November Mayor Lanier's office and the Housing and Community Development department were instrumental in connecting PRH with the Amoco Corporation volunteer effort, an ongoing relationship that has been beneficial to PRH. Again in the Spring of 1994 the mayor assisted PRH in securing a $5,000 grant from the Mayor's Cultural Arts Council, which continues to be a supporter of Project Row Houses.

In other ways, however, the relationship with the City has been problematic. Based in part upon the strength of the City commitment for Community Development Block Grant (CDBG) funds, in September 1993 PRH entered into a lease/purchase agreement with the owner of the row houses. In the months following, however, instead of CDBG funds, PRH received notice that the row houses were on the City's "dangerous buildings" list and that the City was going to tear them down. Ultimately PRH was able to rescue the houses from this fate, but the relationship between PRH and the Department of Housing and Community Development had been seriously damaged. Much of the ensuing battle between the two was played out in the press, which led to a polarization between PRH and the City government. In the end, PRH did not receive CDBG funds, and the purchase of the property was arranged instead through a loan from the Heimbinder Foundation, leaving PRH understandably distrustful of the City's intentions.

Representatives from the Department of Housing and Community Development indicated that the change in identity of PRH from an arts project to a young mothers residential project was problematic from a funding perspective, clouding the identity and direction of the project. Kenneth Bolton, Assistant Director of Housing and Community Development, indicated that the City is still "waiting" for PRH to stabilize. Bolton further suggested that since PRH had ultimately managed to get the funds to purchase the property elsewhere, City support at that level might no longer be needed. At the same time Bolton indicated that the City has recently received over $20,000,000 to spend in areas such as the Third Ward, which is an Enhanced Enterprise Zone, and that they would be open to future proposals from PRH. He did acknowledge that the bureaucratic process can be slow and cumbersome, however, and sometimes difficult to mesh with agendas and schedules of nonprofit entities.

Jessica Cussick, Public Art and Urban Design Director of the Cultural Arts Council of Houston and Harris County, whose organization has provided support to PRH since its inception, was extravagant in her praise of PRH and what it is doing from an arts and cultural perspective. She felt that PRH is unique and enjoys an almost "symbiotic" relationship with the Third Ward community and provides "art, child care and vegetables," in a fully integrated way. She told us about a local African-American bus driver, who passes PRH on his daily route, stopping his bus to inform his riders about the row houses, and the programs and art work which are available there.

City Councilman Jew Don Boney, an African-American Councilman representing the adjacent Fourth Ward, was also outspoken in his praise for PRH. He indicated that conventional development would never have preserved the row houses, and cited their importance and historical origins in West Africa. He felt strongly that the mix of uses on the site represented a true model of community building, and felt that PRH had become an integral part of the fabric of the Third Ward community. He cited the fact that

Houston Councilman Jew Don Boney

PRH, whose doors are open and unlocked, has never had an incident of vandalism because they have earned community trust.

Councilman Boney also cited the importance and quality of the artwork that has been displayed in the Gallery Houses. He felt that the Sacred Geometry exhibit had made a lasting impression on neighborhood residents, and had drawn a mix of people into the area. He noted that both Anglo and Hispanic artists had been included in PRH and felt this was good for the community. He emphasized the importance of introducing art that community residents would not otherwise see, especially art which offers African-Americans various interpretations of their culture. He felt PRH has revitalized the neighborhood, and he recognized the need for someone at the City level to "marry" the funding categories to the PRH approach in order to better support the project.

Organization and Leadership

From its beginning, when Rick Lowe was working in relative isolation toward a personal vision, PRH has grown into a thriving organization. As Founding Director, Rick Lowe continues to define and strengthen the vision of PRH, particularly with respect to the art program. Executive Director Deborah Grotfeldt also oversees activities pertaining to programs, funding, legal issues, administration and organization. Additional staff is now involved in managing the YMRP and other PRH programs. Major funders with whom we spoke mentioned that they were comfortable in contributing to PRH because they had confidence in Lowe and Grotfeldt.

Other significant leadership resides in the Board of Directors. The creation of the Board in 1994 was a critical step, as it has brought together leaders from the Houston business and art community in support of PRH. The board includes business leaders, attorneys, neighborhood leaders, and representatives of Houston's major art institutions, all of whom have lent their professional expertise and/or financial support to the program. The Board is sufficiently diverse to include people with experience in both the arts and in social programming, giving it a valuable depth of expertise.

Project Row Houses Today: The Components of the Project

Eight Gallery Houses: The Art Program

The nature and quality of the art displayed in the Gallery Houses, and the relationship of the artists to the Third Ward community, are central to understanding Project Row Houses. PRH brings art to the community with the objective of engaging people where they are— and for many residents it is their first contact with art. Seven houses provide gallery spaces where regional and national artists are commissioned to work for a six month period to create some specific work, and make themselves available to the community for workshops and interactive discussions. The eighth house, the Project Gallery, provides short term exhibition space for community artists. The first show in Project Gallery House fea-

Deborah Grotfeldt, Executive Director, and Rick Lowe, Founder

Silver Medal: Project Row Houses — 1997 Rudy Bruner Award for Urban Excellence

An early installation entitled "Tribal Markings" by Floyd Newsum included the exterior of the gallery house.

tured the work of 17 year old Angelbert Metoyer, who worked with PRH artists to develop a portfolio which resulted in scholarship offers to several major art schools.

Artists are selected on the merit of their work and their plans for interaction with the community. Each artist creates an art statement within the house—sometimes hanging a show, sometimes creating a total environment which may even include the exterior of the house. In addition, each artist schedules a series of workshops during which the artist interacts with local residents. PRH tries to have a range of artists in each round, including at least one nationally or internationally known artist, one or two from the broader region, and others from the local community. The artists develop installations and cultural activities for adults and youth, including neighborhood teenagers who are sometimes paid to serve as artist's assistants and tour docents. Each artist receives a stipend of $2,000 plus $500 for materials and travel.

Jessica Cussick at the Cultural Arts Council underscored the

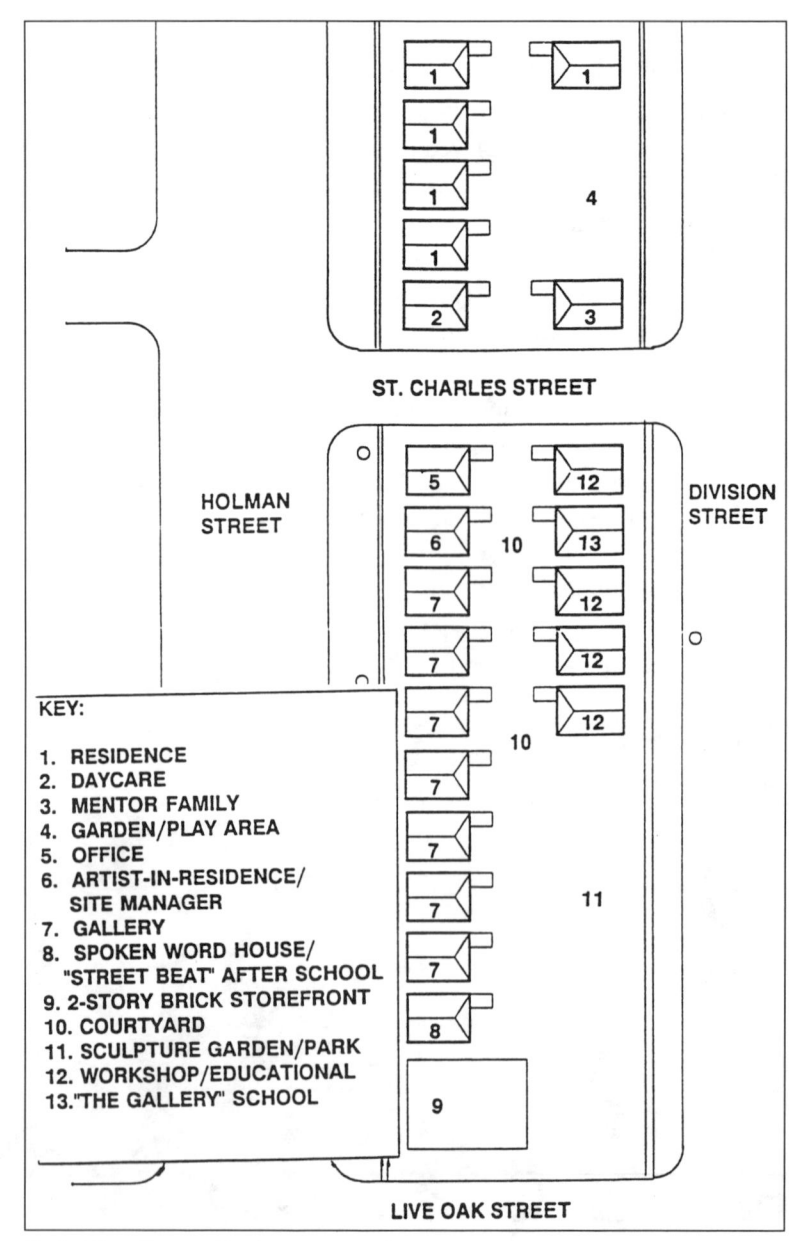

KEY:
1. RESIDENCE
2. DAYCARE
3. MENTOR FAMILY
4. GARDEN/PLAY AREA
5. OFFICE
6. ARTIST-IN-RESIDENCE/ SITE MANAGER
7. GALLERY
8. SPOKEN WORD HOUSE/ "STREET BEAT" AFTER SCHOOL
9. 2-STORY BRICK STOREFRONT
10. COURTYARD
11. SCULPTURE GARDEN/PARK
12. WORKSHOP/EDUCATIONAL
13. "THE GALLERY" SCHOOL

Project Row Houses site plan

fact that people from the Houston arts community and others throughout the City regularly attend events and exhibitions at PRH. She also stated that PRH attracts "fabulous" artists and "has been consistently uncompromising about the quality of art they exhibit; that is a real strength of the project. People are seeing "tough art" which makes them think."

It is integral to the concept of PRH that the art displayed and installed in the Gallery Houses be of high quality, thought provoking, and powerful enough to attract people with many kinds of interests and backgrounds. The installations showcase major contributions of African-American artists to the American art scene, and model African-American achievement. Two PRH artists were subsequently selected for the Whitney Biennial. It is an ambitious agenda that PRH has established, but one which appears to be working.

Detail from Third Ward Archive

Tracey Hicks' installation, "Third Ward Archive," is a photographic record of Third Ward personal histories.

Young Mothers' Residential Program (YMRP)
Located in seven houses down the street from the Gallery Houses, the YMRP provides residences for single mothers between the ages of 17 and 24 and their children for a one year period while they pursue educational goals, work, and learn parenting and life skills. The program includes one day care house, one mentor house, and five residences, each decorated and furnished by a local interior decorator. The residential program was initially conceived of by Deborah Grotfeldt, who saw the need for such a program for young African-American women in the community. Lowe and Grotfeldt brought in Dr. Nelda Lewis, a Third Ward native and PRH neighbor, who holds a MSW and a Ph.D. in child development and family living, to direct the program.

A team of people developed the YMRP concept which is based upon the precept that in order to provide quality care for their children, the young mothers must develop respect for themselves. To be selected for the YMRP, which gives each of the young mothers one of the furnished residences for a one year period, the young women must be enrolled in school and must have jobs, which may be outside PRH or in the office, the day care center or the after-school program.

Sheila Heimbinder, of the Heimbinder Foundation and a PRH Board member, now works on the staff of the YMRP program, evaluating and strengthening the program, with a particular emphasis on expanding the relationship between the program and the Third Ward. She is working with SHAPE Community Center to integrate PRH mothers into the ongoing SHAPE parenting program and, conversely, to invite and include more community mothers in the life skills training offered at PRH.

At the time of the site visit, two of the young mothers were completing their year long program, and three were about halfway through it. The site visit team spent an evening with the young women who spoke about the climate of mutual support in the program and how it allowed them to develop trust, and a sense of community. Each woman felt YMRP had made a major difference in her life; one had made the Dean's list in her pre-med college work at University of Houston and another was learning child care skills working in the YMRP daycare program.

Some of the young mothers currently living at Project Row Houses

Spoken Word House (SWH)

The artist-in-residence at SWH at the time of the visit was African-American video artist Angela Williamston. The house is a media resource center designed to offer opportunity for at-risk youth and adults, and at the same time to provide a support base for multimedia artists who lack resources and facilities to realize their creative vision. SWH houses a music, CD-ROM, and video library as well as a computer, video, and drama production lab. The goal of SWH is to provide a platform for media literacy and community building through exposure to television production and interactive learning.

Angela reported that recently young Latinos who had never been in the Third Ward had been participating in some of the music productions. As she put it, "Music is a universal, colorless language that unites all kinds of people in a groove." Al, a young poet who spoke with us, said the visibility and focus of activity at Spoken Word House was "a pretty cool deal."

One of the YMRP houses, decorated by a local Houston interior designer

Front entry of The Spoken Word House

Sisters in Positive Progress House

This house supports a program designed to address self-esteem and entrepreneurship for African-American women. The House of Nefertiti Gift Shop provides an outlet for sale of crafts produced by neighborhood women, and the house is also a gathering spot for women to discuss cultural and gender issues. Sisters in Positive Progress also sponsors workshops addressing small business development, health, and education.

Day Care

Day care is provided on site for YMRP and for other neighborhood children. Some of the young mothers are employed in the program, and an effort is made to hire Third Ward residents as day care providers.

Street Beat After School/Summer Program

The after-school program serves up to 20 neighborhood children age 6–12. The curriculum is interdisciplinary, and includes tutoring, improved speaking and creative/technical writing skills, African-American history and culture, photography, drum playing, and the like. The goal is to provide the children with individual attention, and to strengthen and reinforce critical thinking skills.

Ted Williams, a neighborhood resident whose children are in the program, spoke about how the children's work in school has improved as a result of the program and what a positive impact the program has had on his community

Community Garden

The community garden is located at the end of the gallery block, behind the houses facing Holman Street. It was launched in collaboration with Urban Harvest, who raised funds to establish the garden where five houses had been torn down. PRH hired a Third Ward resident to coordinate planting and maintenance. Produce is available to anyone in the community who wants to harvest it.

Current Projects and Future Plans

PRH has a number of new initiatives in progress and on the drawing board. Acquisition of the corner site is complete and plans to rehabilitate the building are underway. The building will house a coffee house/gathering space for visitors and community residents, additional performing arts space, and offices for the growing PRH staff.

In addition, the acquisition of vacant land behind the YMRP is now being completed, through the combination of a loan from the Heimbinder Family Foundation, and a charitable contribution of a portion of land cost by the present owner. This site will accommodate additional housing which is being designed on an updated row house model by Nonya Grenader's Rice University Workshop, whose students will also build one house. There has been preliminary discussion about tailoring this housing to the needs of the local elderly population, or alternatively to artist housing. However it is used, this housing is intended to provide an income stream for PRH.

The long-term goal of PRH is to continue to add property and programs as feasible, until the bulk of the adjacent vacant properties on the block have been acquired. Some of the program directions which are currently being considered for the future include larger facilities for day care, housing where visiting artists could live on-site and teach in the community for a period of time, housing for older residents who could assist in the day care program, and expanded performance facilities. An improved level of cooperation from the City of Houston will be important to PRH as they move forward, as the City can provide critical assistance in securing vacant tracts of land adjoining the site.

The rapid development and success of PRH has inspired formation of a national organization which will be based at Project Row Houses and which will provide technical assistance to projects interested in utilizing the PRH model. In their own words, "PRH is establishing a national model for reclamation of inner-city neighborhoods with art as a catalyst to stimulate constructive dialogue addressing cultural, educational and social issues." This organization would be eligible for different funding sources than those available to PRH. Dialogue has already begun in four locations: Dallas, the Watts area of Los Angeles, East St. Louis, and Birmingham. The Dallas project involves development of community exhibit space at the Juanita Craft Museum. The Watts House Project is oriented to renovation of residential units surrounding Watts Towers for living and working space for artists. In East St. Louis African-American dancer-choreographer Katherine Dunham is seeking to establish an arts center involving local historic buildings, and in Birmingham the challenge is to develop a cultural arts complex with artist-in-residence programs in another area of row houses. PRH has recently approached the Rockefeller Foundation for funding for the national initiative.

The dilapidated building adjacent to Project Row Houses was recently purchased.

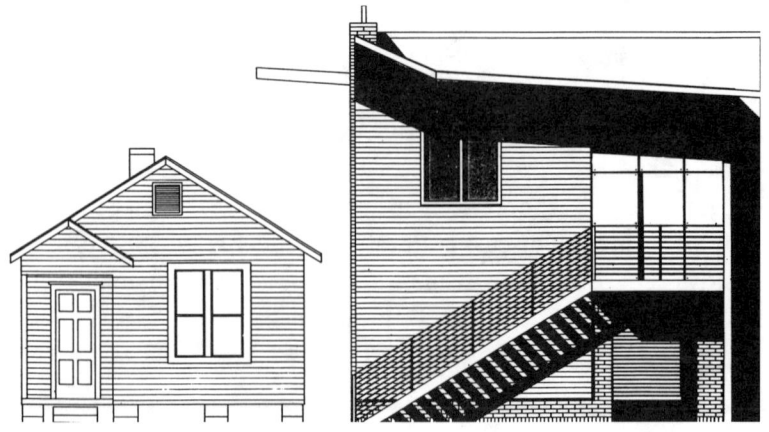

Plans for a new performing arts and community meeting space that will replace the corner building.

Assessing Project Success

How Well Project Row Houses is Meeting its own Goals

The initial goal of PRH was to exhibit the work of African-American artists in order to reconnect their art with the African-American community, contributing to community revitalization. The art program has been established and is now in its fourth round of artist installations, having displayed the work of 32 artists in all, 30 of whom are African-American. The artwork, together with the community workshops, is serving an educational purpose and strengthening the community's identification with its African-American heritage. PRH has attracted artists with national reputations.

PRH has shown the ability to identify and respond to the Third Ward and has established programs which support the community. The evolution of PRH reflects an ability to remain flexible and to establish quality programs as the need arises. It will be important for PRH, however, to establish and maintain priorities, as there are many community issues and needs which must remain beyond the scope of the project.

Response to Selection Committee Questions and Concerns

- *Does PRH change the community vision of itself? Does the Third Ward now feel like a special place?*

  PRH has clearly made an effort to become an integral part of the Third Ward. Relationships with SHAPE Community Center and the Trinity Baptist church are strong, and current residents attest to the good effect it has had on the neighborhood. Former Third Ward residents who have become community leaders are now board members and have become re-involved in the neighborhood through PRH. Dr. Lewis, and Board President James England, both of whom are Third Ward natives, speak with excitement about the positive effect of PRH on their old neighborhood. A new spirit of pride and excitement in what has long been a neglected neighborhood is exemplified by the neighborhood resident and transit worker who stops his bus at PRH to call it to the attention of his passengers.

  PRH alone, however, is not capable of solving the complex problems of the Third Ward. By continuing to strengthen the cultural identity and pride of place in the neighborhood, however, it could well become a catalyst for other revitalization. On its modest scale PRH is making an important contribution to the character and self-image of the Third Ward.

- *Is PRH a real place, not just a display?*

  The architectural integrity of the row houses has been preserved, and they remain modest in scale and level of finish. While the art program attracts many visitors to the site, the residential, day care, and after-school programs make PRH a real, working place, and further integrate it into the community.

- *How has PRH affected the business community?*

  PRH has interacted with the business community in two ways. It has secured the active participation and support of civic and business leaders who serve on the PRH board, contributing time and financial support. The board includes individuals from the corporate and financial sectors, the legal profession, and local government, as well as the arts community.

  In addition, Amoco and Chevron have "adopted" PRH as part of their corporate giving programs, continuing to offer significant ongoing volunteer support, amounting to over one hundred thousand dollars in "in kind services" annually. PRH depends upon the efforts of these volunteers to accomplish much of its building and rehabilitation work and to provide ongoing maintenance. Through this effort, volunteers from many other communities have been introduced to the neighborhood.

- *Who is walking down the street? What is the feeling of the neighborhood?*
The Third Ward is a residential area with several important centers of activity, including PRH, SHAPE Community Center, Trinity United Methodist Church and several retail streets at its edges. Housing is run down, and other evidence of unemployment is visible. Nevertheless, the one story wood houses with mature trees and plantings add character and make the neighborhood feel welcoming.

  The streets around PRH are peopled by a mix of adults, children, and older residents, as well as visitors to PRH. In a community that is 98% African-American, residents are becoming accustomed to the relatively new phenomenon of visitors from other communities arriving at PRH. People from all over Houston and beyond come to see the gallery installations and to meet well known artists, making PRH and the Third Ward a significant art destination in Houston.

- *How real are they? Is this one person's vision or is there an organization growing here?*
Initially, PRH was the vision of Rick Lowe who conceived and manages the art program. With the hiring of Deborah Grotfeldt, the appointment of the board of directors, and the addition of the Young Mothers' Program, PRH has evolved and is now "owned" by a diverse and committed group of professionals and supporters. Staff, board members, people in city government including the mayor, the corporate world, and the Third Ward community all take pride in their involvement with PRH.

- *Is the project financially stable?*
PRH operates on a relatively short funding horizon, and its board recognizes their vulnerability in this respect. On the other hand, PRH has been effective in procuring the funding it needs to sustain itself and to grow. Several hundred thousand dollars have been received in grants from various foundations, and an additional $130,000 in loans from the Heimbinder Foundation. Despite operating costs which are growing as programs expand, PRH has a secure funding base for the upcoming year.

  Plans include development of housing which is intended to provide a modest but steady revenue stream to the project. As PRH grows and evolves, it will be critical to develop additional sources of long term funding and to begin to develop a source of stable investment capital in order to assure project security.

- *Is the project connected to a network of support in the community? In City government? In the business community?*
PRH depends for support upon a network of philanthropic and nonprofit funding entities, some providing renewable funding sources, others one-time grants. Among its major supporters are the Cultural Arts Council of Houston, the NEA, the Houston Endowment, and the Heimbinder Foundation. Corporations such as Amoco, Chevron, MASCO, and US Homes have provided significant volunteer and financial support. The relationship to City government is clearly more complex. The Cultural Arts Council of Houston and Harris County has been a staunch supporter, providing grants over the course of several years. As of the date of the site visit, the Department of Housing and Community Development had not provided funds, despite early indication of their intention to do so.

  The art community in Houston, including the major museums and the Menil collection, has been consistently supportive, and has sponsored restoration of several gallery houses.

- *What are the spin-offs and current and future plans? Where are they going next? What are they doing in Watts and East St. Louis?*
PRH has extensive plans for the future. Design and construction assistance has been procured for the new performing arts/coffee bar building on the corner. Adjacent land next to the

YMRP is under agreement, and designs are proceeding for new housing for the elderly and visiting artists. Acquisition of additional land is being actively discussed, and city assistance is being sought. PRH is also lending expertise to other inner-city neighborhoods who wish to use art as catalyst to stimulate community revitalization. Initiatives in Birmingham, Alabama; Los Angeles; and East St. Louis are currently underway. (See Future Plans.)

Impact on Neighborhood and Community

PRH has a multi-layered relationship with the Third Ward. The diversity of programming, from the Gallery Houses to the Young Mothers program, has served to involve many different age groups. In addition, PRH has made an effort to hire Third Ward residents when possible.

Board member James England, Head of Litigation for the Metropolitan Transit Authority, is a Third Ward native who lends his legal expertise to the project. As a former resident of the area, Mr. England feels PRH had been "tremendously important" for the neighborhood. He noted that it was remarkable that with computers, fax machines and other expensive equipment in the project, it had never been vandalized or burglarized.

Values Reflected in PRH and its Development Processes

PRH grew out of the desire on the part of African-American artists led by Rick Lowe to reconnect their art to the African-American community. That remains the underlying mission of the arts program at PRH. Other programs such as the Young Mothers' Residential Program have evolved in response to PRH's commitment to retain the flexibility to respond to community needs, and reflect an expanded sense of mission and values.

Leadership Effectiveness

Rick Lowe's vision and Deborah Grotfeldt's skill in administration and fund-raising have taken PRH from vision to reality, creating an arts center, a transitional housing program, and a center for day care, after-school care and entrepreneurial training and development. Together Lowe and Grotfeldt have overcome considerable obstacles and made PRH into an innovative center, true to its original goals. PRH is growing, however, and it is no longer feasible to have only two people run it. Third Ward residents are currently being trained to manage many of the day-to-day activities.

The Board of Directors for PRH is dedicated and extremely active. The Board has representation from the corporate, philanthropic, and political sectors, and is ready and willing to provide PRH with policy direction, fund-raising support, and financial oversight. The long-term viability of PRH is enhanced by the involvement and expertise at the Board level.

"Echo" by Whitfield Lovell features charcoal drawings suggesting early row house residents.

Prospects for Sustainability

While the project has grown and now seems relatively stable, it is by no means secure. Up to now, PRH has been successful in attracting funds to purchase the row house property and to operate an array of programs in a relatively small physical space. As PRH gains momentum and a demonstrated history, its ability to attract funding may improve. In addition, it appears likely that the City of Houston will work with PRH to help them access funds available for neighborhood revitalization. The increased visibility of the project in Houston has also set the stage for upcoming fund-raising programs, including extending sponsorship to include all 22 houses and the staging of a gala evening event sponsored by the Board.

In order to reduce its dependence on annually renewed and one-time sources of "soft money," PRH hopes that new housing will provide a modest income stream, as will future expansion schemes. The formation of a separate entity through which PRH will work in other locations throughout the country to help municipalities and start-up projects adapt the PRH model is another potential source of income in the long term, and has already attracted the attention of the Rockefeller Foundation. In the final analysis, however, as more short term goals continue to be realized, a long term goal of the project will be to develop an endow-

Gallery House block with future performing arts space and courtyard behind

ment or source of capital which will provide long-term financial security for Project Row Houses.

Selection Committee Comments

Project Row Houses was recognized by every member of the Selection Committee as an innovative and important project. There was a strong feeling that PRH raised important issues about the place of art in community revitalization, in building pride in African-American artistic accomplishment, and the potential of art in engaging different groups of people across traditional barriers.

The fact that PRH has made the city establishment "uncomfortable" was considered by the Selection Committee to be an asset for two reasons. On the one hand, it was felt that the discomfort arose in part from the fact that PRH was a true grass roots organization, operating outside the accepted channels of government process. This fact relates to its broad community support and the flexibility and responsiveness that the project has maintained, allowing it to change and respond to community needs.

The committee also felt that the tension with the city was due in part to PRH's unique blend of art, art-based workshops, Young Mothers' Residential Program, and other programs, which together did not conform to any pre-established funding slots and implicitly challenged traditional urban revitalization funding practices. This suggests an innovative model which may well be ahead of traditional funding patterns in its approach to urban problems.

The simple physical beauty of Project Row Houses was also commended by the committee. One member noted that the she was happy to see that buildings that would not normally be preserved had been restored in a way that was respectful of their classical proportions and architectural integrity. She felt it would have been easy to diminish the aesthetic quality of the buildings

Holman Street elevation of Young Mothers Residential Program houses

because they are small, but instead a remarkable and beautiful place had been created.

Most of the questions about PRH related to its relative newness. While all of the project components, especially the art project, were commended for their originality and potential in community revitalization, the committee felt it was too early to judge the lasting impact of PRH and its programs. The image used by the committee is that it is still a bit fragile, a "butterfly," and that the lasting effects of Project Row Houses will become clear in time.

Detail from "The Third Ward Archive"

For more information

Project Row Houses
2501 Holman Street
Houston, TX 77004

TEL: 713-526-7662

WEB SITE: www.projectrowhouses.com

silver MEDAL 1997

RUDY BRUNER AWARD FOR URBAN EXCELLENCE

Hismen Hin-nu
Oakland, California

Hismen Hin-Nu at a Glance

What is Hismen Hin-Nu?
- A mixed use development with 92 units of housing for low income residents and 14,000 square feet of retail space on a main commercial artery in a transitional neighborhood.

Who Made the Submission?
- East Bay Asian Local Development Corporation (EBALDC – pronounced "Eee-Bald-Cee"). The project's co-sponsor is the San Antonio Community Development Corporation.

Major Goals and Accomplishments of Hismen Hin-Nu
- To transform an underutilized site into an attractive, mixed use project.
- To build experience and encourage cooperation among local community developers.
- To improve the immediate neighborhood.
- To integrate multi-cultural art into the project.
- To complete construction at reasonable cost and within budget
- To achieve full occupancy and successful operation in both residential and retail operations.

Reasons For Including Hismen Hin-Nu as a Finalist
- Exemplary for small scale community development project;
- Good design process and site assembly;
- Use of local contractors;
- Appears to have good ethnic mix.

Selection Committee Questions and Concerns for Site Visit
- Who lives in the project, how diverse is the population, and how do they get along (e.g., various ethnic groups or life stages)?
- Were/are residents drawn from a pool of local applicants or did they come from outside the area? How are tenants selected? Screening? Criteria?
- Is the commercial space occupied? Working well?
- The submission admits to a lack of usable open space. What is done to compensate for that, either by the project or the residents?
- What is the impact of the project on the neighborhood and vice versa?
- Were local contractors used in construction?
- What is the quality of the design, including image and appearance, artwork, etc.? Do residents and neighbors perceive the place as being special?
- What is the quality and durability of materials? Are details appropriate or too elaborate? Is maintenance (and its budget) adequate?

Hismen Hin-nu from International Way, formerly East 14th Street

- What special resources were applied to the project (University of California at Berkeley or others) and how were they used? What did they contribute?
- Have any follow-up studies (e.g., a post-occupancy evaluation) been done?

Final Selection Committee Comments

- The participatory planning process, collaboration between two community development organizations, and the architectural design were considered exemplary.
- The project was the work of a mature and effective organization, (EBALDC).
- The Committee speculated that some additional pre-development work on the issue of retail design and mix might have benefited the retail component of the project.

Project Description

Chronology

1988 Architecture and planning students from several schools, under the direction of Michael Pyatok (later the design architect for the project), study the development potential of sites along East 14th Street and identify this one, among others, as underutilized with good potential for a dense, mixed use project. Findings are reported to the city.

1990 EBALDC purchases the property with the help of the city and forms a partnership with the San Antonio Community Development Corporation, which has stronger roots in the neighborhood, for its development.

1991 Design workshops are held under the auspices of the San Antonio CDC.

1993 Construction starts in July.

1995 Construction completed in March.

Key Participants *(persons interviewed are indicated by an asterisk*)*

Lynette Jung Lee,* *Executive Director of EBALDC*
Joshua Simon,* *Senior Project Manager of EBALDC*
Ted Dang,* *member of EBALDC board and local realtor and property manager*
Vince Reyes,* *chair of EBALDC board*
Don "Little Cloud" Davenport,* *Executive Director of San Antonio Community Development Corporation*
Eric Cone*, *Board of Directors, San Antonio Community Development Corporation*
Margaret Jackson,* *Resident Property Manager*
Roosevelt Johnson,* *Maintenance Supervisor*
Michael Pyatok,* *(design architect) and The Ratcliff Architects (architects of record).*
Artists: Reynaldo Terrazas* *gates,* Horace Washington *tiles,* Daniel Galvez *mural,* Mia Kodani *frieze panels at tops of towers*
Elnora Gay,* *director of on-site Headstart program*

The Project

Hismen Hin-Nu Terrace is a mixed use, affordable housing and retail project in an ethnically and economically diverse neighborhood of Oakland, California. Hismen Hin-Nu consists of 92 housing units distributed as follows:

Size	Units
1 bedroom	17
2 bedrooms	35
3 bedrooms	30
4 bedrooms	10

The considerable number of larger units responds to the needs of families, including multigenerational ones, in this area. In addition to the housing, there are about 14,000 square feet of commercial space which includes a larger retail area (with a convenience market), a market hall for smaller merchants, some stalls along the street (which were abandoned after the site visit), and a Headstart school. There is also a community meeting room and some office space for the property managers. Due to its rather high density, and the city's requirement for a significant amount of parking, the housing is built over a parking garage.

At Hismen Hin-Nu, the largest tenant group is African-Americans (64%), followed by Asian-Pacific Islanders (21%) and Latinos (13%); Caucasians make up only about 2%. Tenants report that they get along well together and that the racial mix has not resulted in conflicts.

Income levels at Hismen Hin-Nu show 44% earning less than 30% of median income with another 43% earning between 31% and 50% of median income. This is less skewed toward the lowest income residents than other EBALDC projects (where 56% to 100% of tenants have incomes below 30% of median). Generally, the income mix is dictated by requirements of the funding program (such as low income tax shelters).

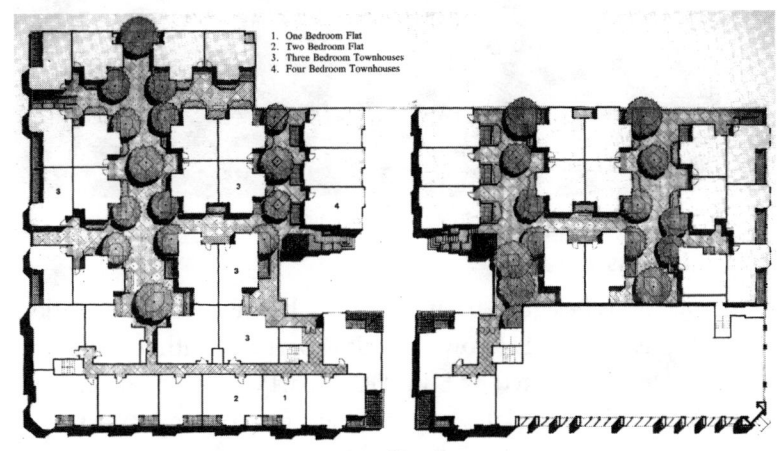

Plan of Hismen Hin-nu at upper courtyard level

Project Origin

Identifying and Obtaining the Site

Well before the project started, the site was identified as one among several with potential for supporting this type and scale of mixed use project. This finding came from a study conducted for the city by a group of students from U.C. Berkeley and other schools led by the architect, Michael Pyatok, who eventually became the project's designer. Following this report, EBALDC did a feasibility study showing that a viable project could be built there.

The site was a vacant supermarket which had been the subject of a foreclosure auction. The Oakland City Council and Redevelopment Agency agreed to fund a loan to EBALDC to purchase the property, though a competing proposal for a new supermarket was also being considered. At the auction, the supermarket chain started with their high bid ($950,000) and allowed EBALDC to buy the property for only $100 more without bidding again. EBALDC acquired the building and parking lot, which covered a half block – just under one and one-half acres. Prior to building the new project, EBALDC operated an indoor "flea market" there, many of whose vendors later relocated to the new building.

The Neighborhood

East 14th Street is a prominent and busy commercial artery which connects downtown Oakland to many of its southerly neighborhoods. Along its length, there are areas that are highly mixed and in transition; some are run down and some are bustling with activity.

In the immediate vicinity are housing, retail, commercial, and fast food outlets. There is another rather dense mixed-use project directly across 14th Street, built by the San Antonio CDC, a partner in Hismen Hin-Nu. Just across the street to the west (behind Hismen Hin-Nu) is an elevated rapid transit line (BART). Toward the south lies the Fruitvale neighborhood, a lively area which is largely Hispanic and the location of the nearest BART station.

Housing in the vicinity is generally in decent to good condition and we saw many pleasant blocks with modest single family houses, duplexes, and moderate-size apartment buildings. Property was described as being too valuable to allow it to deteriorate. We were told that there has been considerable investment in local real estate by recent Asian immigrants. There is reported to be rather little neighborhood open space in the area, with only two parks for 60,000 people.

Standard Brands store adjacent to the site, with Jack-in-the-Box in background

BART track behind Hismen Hin-nu

The Name

The co-sponsoring agency, San Antonio Community Development Corporation, is led by Don Davenport, a member of the Seminole tribe. He assembled the tribal elders who named the project Hismen Hin-Nu which means "Sun Gate" in the language of the Indians native to this area (the Muwekma Ohlone). He reported that the artist selected to design the gate incorporated the sunburst motif based on the name, although the artist recalled that he had already done the gate, which provided the image for the name. This difference in perception suggests broad ownership of the name and design.

The Sun Gate itself serves both security and decorative purposes.

Design Process

The project was designed by architect Michael Pyatok, who works locally but is nationally known for his experience with low income housing. He was selected by EBALDC as part of a joint venture with The Ratcliff Associates, another local firm of more substantial size. The design evolved through a participatory process, described in the following paragraphs.

The San Antonio CDC, which was more closely tied than EBALDC to the immediate community, was instrumental in providing the forum for community involvement. Such an approach was said to be a standard part of any planning process they would undertake and is also typical of the way the city, EBALDC, and the design architect work – thus, everyone expected a participatory design process. This process ensures that any opposition will surface, that useful suggestions will be received, and that the neighborhood will endorse the resulting project.

To locate participants, San Antonio sent out fliers and called people they thought would be interested. Many of these were "stakeholders" rather than representatives of future project residents, though some were said to be at similar income levels as future residents.

As many as 50 to 60 people came to some meetings, with approximately 20 to 30 typically attending each of the three design workshops. The workshops were highly structured by the architect in a manner that is more or less standard for him. Much of the work was hands-on, done by smaller groups of up to 10 who would meet for about two hours at each session, using blocks to make models. The workshops covered site design, the living units, and image.

For the site workshop, the architect prepared model kits which allowed participants to explore alternative parking arrangements (e.g., at the unit, away from the unit, or mixed), although the architect already knew that, at over 50 units per acre, it would be necessary to have a parking garage under most units. The small groups worked with the model for about an hour, then presented the advantages and disadvantages of their scheme to the whole group. For parking, the preferred scheme was to have two garages with some ground level open space (and the project was, in fact, designed this way).

Key neighborhood concerns related to the density and scale of the project. Some neighbors were afraid that it might be too massive or have too great an impact on the schools. The project started by testing how to fit 100 units on the site, while some wanted as few as 50 units. All participants liked the plan that grouped units around a series of courtyards. At the second workshop, the teams studied density and massing. They found that if they put the taller building along East 14th (the north side of the site), they got better sunlight into the balance of the project. While some had been concerned about the scale and mass on the street, the decision to put the taller building on East 14th was made by consensus. In the end, the group was comfortable that the 92 units would fit properly on the site and in the neighborhood.

Many other important design decisions were aired and resolved at the workshops, including the location of various elements, how to handle access, and where to place entries. The architect's perception is that participants compromised, accepting the plan for one main entry (even though many had advocated multiple entrances) since, once inside, the design divided the project in two, reducing the number of people who would share each open space.

Don Davenport and Eric Cone of San Antonio Community Development Corporation

The final workshop dealt with image; here the architect showed slides of many apartment houses of similar size from the area. These included Craftsman and Mission styles, with the latter particularly liked by participants because it reflects the history of the area. This greatly influenced the actual design, as the architect felt that he could work in almost any relevant architectural style (see next section).

EBALDC also does a "post-occupancy evaluation" (assessment of the success of the project after it is occupied) of each project to gain insights for future work. They cited many examples of things they had learned from a recent project, many of which were incorporated into or improved upon at Hismen Hin-Nu. One finding indicated the need for excellent visibility into the laundry room – thus, large windows were provided. The documentation that EBALDC provided, while valuable and insightful, was more an audit of the process and the achievement of organizational goals than an assessment of the design. There was no feedback from tenants, nor was the architect involved. On the other hand, the audit reported that the project met or exceeded many goals (e.g., for minority and local hiring during construction) and had many useful suggestions for improving project management.

Design

For the architect, a key design challenge was how to break down the massive scale and potentially monolithic appearance of a project that is over 400 feet long and four stories tall at the street. This was done through subdividing the mass (dividing the length and giving relief with vertical elements and trellised balconies). Red tile roofs on portions of the project and a variety of colors (selected with the clients) further define these elements. The principal finishing materials are stucco and cement fiber siding.

There is a carefully planned hierarchy of open spaces which is intended to both limit and reinforce social interactions. The

Residential courtyard at upper level

Central interior courtyard

residential areas have a single, central entrance from the street which gives access to a shared space treated as a symbolic town square where all residents meet on their way in and out. In this space are mailboxes and shared facilities such as the manager's office, laundry, and community meeting room. From here, there are four other entries: two give access to the elevators serving the smaller apartments and two give access to the stairs serving the family-oriented townhouses. The townhouses, with no more than 20 on each side, share an upper level courtyard intended for use by small children. These spaces do, indeed, present the feeling of an urban street, with entrances and frequent activity.

Pyatok, the architect, says that as a result of efforts to break down the building's scale and mass, they ended up with 25 different plans for housing units – a lot of work in design, but offering considerable variety and choice in living arrangements. In some larger units the intent is to accommodate multi-generational families, with a bedroom on the ground floor for grandparents who might have difficulty with stairs. Many units were able to have balconies, in part because FHA standards, which would have severely limited them, did not apply to this project – and such niceties were affordable within the budget.

The dwellings themselves are well-liked by tenants we talked to (we visited three or four and spoke with others). They found them to be spacious, liked the abundant cabinets, and the balconies were appreciated and reported to be used.

Retail Design

A Headstart facility and retail spaces are located on the ground floor, with direct access from the street, on either side of the main residential entrance. The retail component consists of one larger store which is at one corner (occupied by a family-run business called Dollars and More), a market hall for up to 140 smaller merchants at the other corner, and five niches along the street facade.

There is a separate portion of the parking garage dedicated to the retail area; it is used mostly by the vendors themselves and for service access rather than for customer parking.

During the planning phase, merchants wanted only one entrance to the market hall, partly for security. The architect, however, feared that would kill the street and so suggested street niches for vendors, setting the glass back five feet. While this gives excellent exposure to those vendors, it blocks the view of the market hall interior. There were many discussions about having roll down doors for these vendors. A trip to Pike Place market in Seattle (which does not have them) confirmed for the vendors that they wanted the roll downs so they could leave their merchandise in place and be sure it was safe. The merchants also wanted the main entrance to the market hall to be close to the intersection that had two fast food restaurants (though one was closed at the time of our visit). After our site visit, the vendor stalls were vacated (in part to give the rest of the merchants better visibility from the street), the vendors relocated to underutilized space inside, and a second door was opened into the market hall.

Street vending stalls on East 14th Street

PROJECT ORGANIZATION

- 4 bedroom townhomes
- 3 bedroom townhomes
- 1 & 2 bedroom flats

- Side Residential Entry
- Residential Parking
- Retail Parking
- Shops
- Child Care
- MAIN RESIDENTIAL ENTRY
- Community Center
- Street Vendors
- MARKET HALL
- Side Residential Entry
- Residential Parking
- Retail Parking

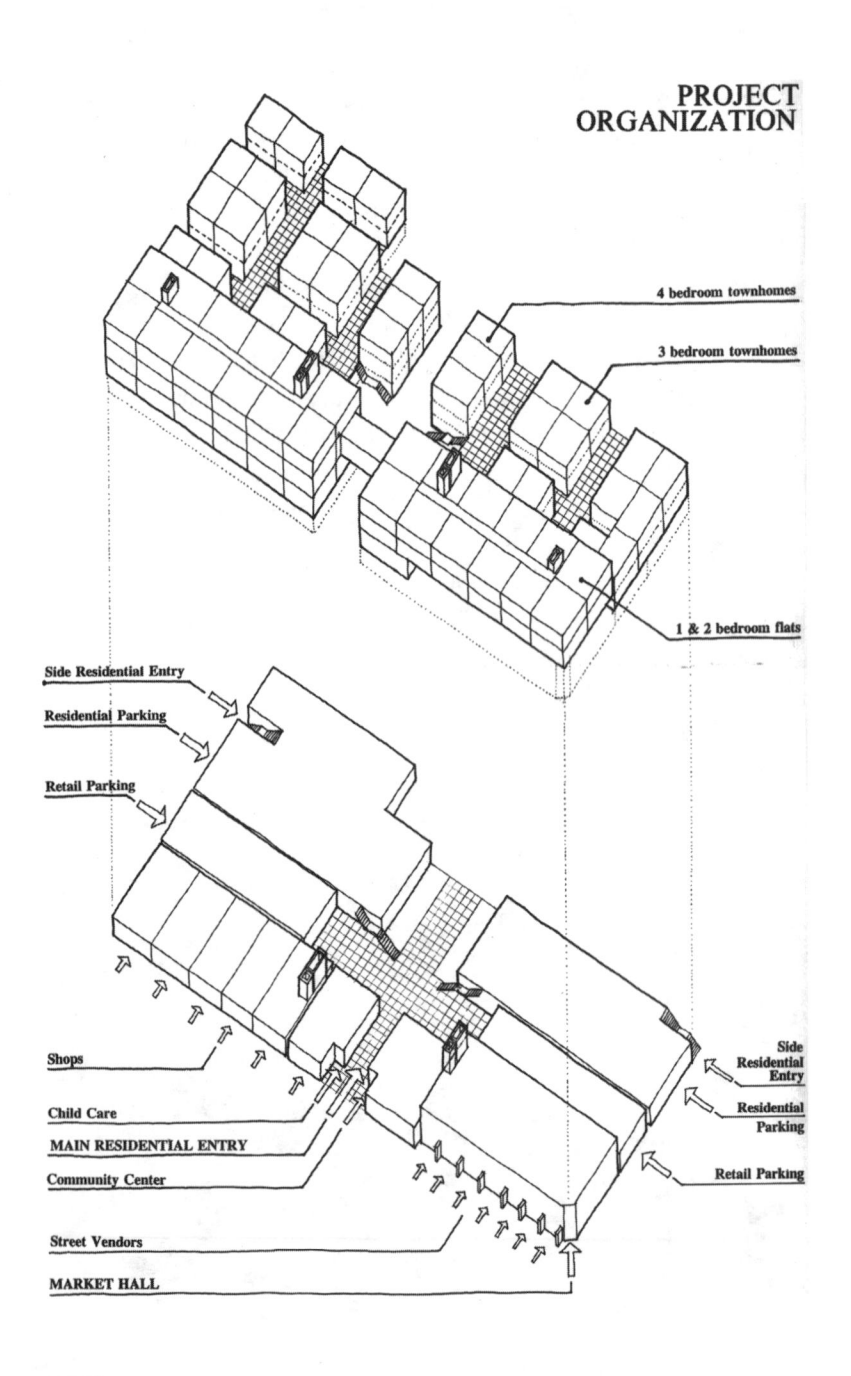

Design Details and Maintenance

Overall, design and construction are of high quality and an active maintenance program has kept the project in good condition, a fact well appreciated by tenants with whom we spoke. An example of good detailing is the provision of oak wainscoting in the community meeting room, which otherwise would undoubtedly have shown wear and tear from its high level of use. Other quality features are the programmable central locking system and the appliances, which have required little maintenance. The feature most liked by tenants is the bay window with bench that is provided in many units. Tenants report that they sit and watch the street from these windows (and also from balconies in other units).

There are some minor problems including staining and mildew on some stucco surfaces, which may be a problem with the paint. There have also been minor problems with the water-conserving toilets because tenants have had to learn to hold the handles down when they flush. At the interior corridor, hall lights had to be changed from open sconces to closed fixtures because children had thrown debris into them. Some of the added maintenance is the result of wear and tear due to having twice the anticipated number of children. Despite this fact, maintenance costs appear to be reasonable.

There is also a very active maintenance program directed at removing graffiti. The resident maintenance manager tours the building each morning and has any graffiti removed that same morning so that the appearance is never allowed to deteriorate.

Art in Architecture

A hallmark of this project is the incorporation of art into the design. This was the architect's concept and he spearheaded a successful effort to get $50,000 from the National Endowment for the Arts. His intent was to use the art not only as decoration, but to symbolize the racial and cultural diversity and unity of the area.

To that end, he invited artists representing various racial groups to submit portfolios and participated in their selection with EBALDC. He says: "The coexistence of art from these diverse traditions inspires a spirit of cooperation not only among the tenants but in the community." Examples of this expression include Mia Kodani's frieze panels at tops of the towers which weave together patterns from many cultures, and the tiles by Horace Washington which represent 22 distinct cultures, some of which are African.

We met with Reynaldo Terrazas, artist of the sunburst gate and entry arch. He is a local sculptor and this was his first public art commission. His charge in designing the gate was to provide an image that could be appropriate and inclusive to the entire community, as well as lending physical security. He appears to have provided a highly imageable solution (see The Name, above).

Mia Kodani's freize at entrance

Reynaldo Terrazas, artist and neighborhood resident, standing at the Sun Gate he designed.

Accommodating Children

As stated above, there are twice the anticipated number of children living in the project, in a neighborhood which suffers from a lack of recreational space. The project houses 54 children aged five and under and 100 aged six through 17.

In theory, the spaces provided for children include both the ground-level central courtyard and the upper level courtyards in front of the townhouse units for younger children (under five). While the upper level spaces are close to parents, they are of irregular configuration, broken up by planters, and not very easy to supervise. Children over about five years old can use play equipment shared with Headstart in the central courtyard on the street level. We also saw a few kids riding bikes in this area, but there is not much space available for this activity. There is really no provision for teens, but EBALDC hopes to obtain the use of an adjacent empty lot for basketball and "hang out" space. It would be possible to gain direct access to this space by cutting a hole in a rear wall; this would go a long way toward solving the problem.

Hismen Hin-Nu from International Boulevard (formerly E. 14th Street)

Retail Operations

The 8,000 square feet of retail space was fully leased at opening, but is currently only 60% occupied (about 3,200 square feet are vacant). Merchants have faced a variety of challenges, many related to general changes in retailing as well as to changes in the immediate area. Sales volume at Dollars and More, the largest single tenant, was reported to have dropped 40% since opening and there were rumors that it was likely to be closing in the near future.

While 14th Street is major commercial thoroughfare, a new Kmart, McFrugal's, and a large supermarket opened six months after Hismen Hin-Nu and only about a mile away, drawing potential customers away. In addition, a paint store next door went bankrupt and is empty, further reducing the traffic volume. It has now been replaced by a 98¢ store which sells the same goods as the Dollars & More store located in the Hismen Hin-nu development. While this is a transitional time and place, there are other projects which will eventually help to improve the situation, including the redevelopment of a large parcel a few blocks away.

According to the architect, the retail space is "an experiment that will evolve." EBALDC had more retail experience than most non-profits, and is gaining more through this project. The architect describes the space as "flexible and correctable." If given the opportunity to redesign it from scratch, he would not separate the retail elements, but would centralize them for greater synergy and flexibility.

The site visit team spent some time in the store, "Elle's," operated by EBALDC. It is run with help from their retail specialist (DeLynda DeLeon) who trains staff and oversees operations by visiting about three times per week. Elle's is a women's clothing shop opened in response to requests. It employs (and trains) three EBALDC residents, two of whom are from Hismen Hin-Nu. Open since Christmas, when it did more business, it was just breaking even (and had not yet started paying rent) at the time of RBA's visit. Capital and operating shortfalls are covered by EBALDC's other profit-making ventures.

The tenant employee we interviewed described the importance to her of this opportunity. In recovery from drug abuse, lacking even a GED, and the mother of a 15 year old, this is her first job. She has real responsibilities, is learning a great deal about retailing, and now has another part time job at one of the other shops. She could not say enough in praise of the program and the positive impact it has had on her self-esteem. She now gets dressed up every day, is trusted, is very active as a tenant and uses the special services that are offered (she's a Home Alert captain, takes budgeting classes, and so forth).

Parking

Eighty-three residential and 30 interior retail parking spaces are provided to satisfy city requirements, representing a negotiated reduction from parking standards. However, there are differences of opinion about the number of parking spaces needed by the project. Some people we interviewed felt that the parking was underutilized because the lower income population served by the project has fewer cars or can't afford California's mandatory insurance (proof of which is required in order to park in the garage).

Pyatok claimed that, in his experience, residents like these have less than one car per unit – he would estimate 0.7 to 0.8 as an appropriate ratio, while the city typically requires one parking space per unit. The project's actual ratio is about 0.85 cars per unit and Pyatok claims that, with a further reduction in parking requirements, it would have been possible to have stoops on the side streets by dropping some of the housing half a floor.

However, the property manager reports that one side of the garage has all its spaces assigned, while the other has only about five spaces available. Spaces are assigned on a first come, first served basis and only one tenant has requested a space when none was available on the side they wanted. Several tenant households appear to own more than one car.

Security

Overall, everyone we talked with (including management, tenants, and the police) felt that the complex was quite, if not perfectly, safe and secure. One mother we interviewed was pleased to have enclosed outdoor space where her younger children can play. She finds it to be safe, especially from vehicular traffic.

There is considerable physical security provided, including lighting, gates, a computerized key card access system, and surveillance cameras. The office is next to, and has a view of, the entrance. Personal security services have been increased greatly since opening and now include weekend coverage. It is operated on contract to a group affiliated with a Black Muslim organization. They are reported to be professional and well trained, respectful, but also streetwise and firm.

A police officer who patrols this area said that they get very few calls to come to Hismen Hin-Nu. While the neighborhood has some crime problems, the officer said that it is located between two improving areas.

There has been some destruction of property, including two doors kicked in, possibly related to drug traffic (these tenants have been evicted — see Management, below). There has also been at least one incident of domestic violence. Overall, that is a very acceptable record for a project of this size and type in its location.

Development Costs

For the **residential** portion of the project (and its parking), the costs were:

Item	Cost
Site Acquisition (with off-site improvements)	$854,829
Construction	$9,994,693
Fees (permits, A/E, inspection)	$1,284,575
General Development Costs (incl. interest, loan fees, insurance)	$1,764,543
Total Development Costs (before syndication costs and dev. fee)	**$13,898,640**
Interest on Tax Credit Bridge Loan	$2,023,481
Syndication Costs	$904,978
Development and Operating Fees	$2,084,550
Total	**$18,911,648**

The architect felt that the construction budget for the residential portion was adequate at about $77 per square foot.

For the **commercial** portion of the project (and its parking), construction costs were approximately $900,000 for the shell plus about $350,000 for tenant improvements. The total development cost for the commercial space was about $1.8 million.

Financing

As is typical of projects of this type, there were many sources of financing, though this project was made somewhat more complex than usual due to its mixed uses. Funds could not be mingled between the residential and commercial portions which, as a result, also had to be physically separated. Complex legal negotiations and documentation were required to establish inter-creditor agreements.

Permanent financing for the residential portion was provided as follows (not including construction period loans or advances against tax credits not yet received):

Residential Financing Source	Amount
Calif. Community Reinvestment Corp.	$1,210,000
State Rental Housing Construction Program	$3,720,386
City of Oakland	$1,775,127
Merritt Community Capital (tax credits)	$3,153,487
Fannie Mae (tax credits)	$8,926,124
Total	**$18,785,124**

For the commercial portion of the project, financing was provided as follows:

Commercial Financing Source	Amount
City of Oakland (CDBG)	$650,000
Ford Foundation	537,346
Irvine Foundation	500,000
EBALDC Investment (From Tax Credit Development Fee)	107,900
Total	**$1,795,246**

In terms of ongoing revenues and expenses, the housing appears to operate within budget, generating a very small distribution to its sponsors. The retail space would operate at close to break even with a lower vacancy rate and is thus still struggling (see section above on Retail Operations). Rents (some including common area charges which also cover utilities) range from $0.82 to $1.15 per square foot per month.

Profile of EBALDC

EBALDC was founded to serve the Asian community in the East Bay. However, it has now expanded its mission to serve low income residents of all races, while retaining part of its focus on the needs of Asians. The Asian community itself has been changing considerably; it was mostly Chinese, but more recently there has been a dramatic increase in Southeast Asian and other Asian populations.

Lynette Jung Lee, Executive Director of EBALDC

EBALDC was formed in 1975 to develop a multi-service center in downtown Oakland (the Asian Resource Center) which now generates cash to subsidize non-profit operations and youth programs. Other EBALDC projects use profits from commercial rents to subsidize such services as a child care center that might get free rent.

EBALDC has considerable development experience, including large scale projects. It owns $75 million worth of real estate and has $2 million in the bank and another $2 million line of credit. Its other current projects and plans include redeveloping a historic market building in downtown Oakland. EBALDC has expanded its organization to include a community planning section which is currently preparing a neighborhood plan for the area. Despite these strong capabilities, EBALDC often works with other organizations, as it did on this project (see the section below on the joint venture with San Antonio).

EBALDC is evolving from property development and management toward economic development, and now has a department dedicated to this function. Its recently prepared long range plan will make economic development its new focus. EBALDC operates its own businesses and invests in others. Among its businesses are property management and construction management, which tap into its core experience. It operates a revolving loan fund for "micro lending" which, working with only $12,000 capitalization, has made 26 loans in 10 years. It also helps individuals and families with personal finances, savings, shopping, and computer orientation. EBALDC uses its own funds to match one-for-one a participant's contributions to a savings plan (called an individual development account).

The Joint Venture

While EBALDC initiated this project, they realized that they lacked strong connections in the immediate neighborhood of the project. As a remedy, they proposed a joint venture with the San Antonio Community Development Corporation. Not only did San Antonio take the lead in organizing the community participation process, but they also assisted with getting Head Start in the building and in getting the city to contribute $650,000 in CDBG funds for the commercial space.

The City's Role

The City of Oakland played an important part in this project. They claim to have conceived of the project (probably referring to an early study done for them by the architect and a team of students in which the site was identified as having the potential for this type of project). They also provided funding for it at an early stage, when they perceived it as still being only partly defined and posing considerable risks. The fact that the city had a long track record with EBALDC and considerable confidence in them allowed the city to offer this support which, in turn, made possible a quick purchase of the property at a favorable price.

Management, Tenant Selection, and Eviction Of Problem Tenants

EBALDC provides full-time on-site management at Hismen Hin-Nu. As part of its agreement with San Antonio CDC, it will train them to take over management in the next few years.

Central to management is a rigorous tenant selection process. There is a long waiting list, a written application, income verification, written contact with the prior landlord, and a home visit. Income is re-certified each year, though the income trend is reported to be generally downward for tenants. Five tenants were evicted when it was discovered that their incomes were above the acceptable limits. One tenant we interviewed had been on the waiting list for a year before getting in, which was said to be typical.

There have been three evictions in 15 months for violations such as drug use or prostitution. In general, if tenants are struggling, management tries to work with and help them to resolve their problems, including establishing a flexible rent payment schedule. Eviction is a last resort.

Detail of freize panel on residential elevation

Social Programs and Supports

There is a considerable number of on-site services available to tenants. Kids' House is an after-school program for 6 to 12 year olds. We visited the program, talked with its director, and saw about 12 kids doing a variety of activities, including reading, doing homework, playing, and having a snack.

Head Start is a rent-paying tenant on the ground floor, with direct street access and use of courtyard play space. It runs two classes of up to 17 children each, for two half-day sessions, serving a total of 68 children. Less than half the children live at Hismen Hin-Nu, though not all of Hismen Hin-Nu's children are able to participate – this depends on their parent's ability to make arrangements for their care for the other half of the day. It is perceived to be an excellent facility, with adequate outdoor space.

Three units at Hismen Hin-Nu are contracted to a program called Shelter Plus Care that provides drug and alcohol treatment as well as aftercare to people who live in the complex. The tenant we interviewed who was working in EBALDC's retail shop was part of this program.

EBALDC also has other programs to help individuals and families including employment and job training (see the list in the section profiling the organization).

Assessing Project Success

How Well It Meets Its Own Goals

- *To provide a substantial, high quality, mixed-use project.*
  It has fully met this goal.
- *To provide supportive services to tenants.*
  Several useful services are provided on site (daycare, Headstart, economic development support), while others are available through EBALDC off site.

How Well It Meets Selection Committee Concerns

- *Who lives in the project, how diverse is the population, and how do they get along?*
  The tenant mix is reflective of the surrounding neighborhood. It is largely African-American, with smaller numbers of Asians and Latinos, and very few whites. Tenants report that the ethnic groups all get along well together.

- *Is the commercial space occupied? Working well?*
  Of the market hall, about 60% is occupied. While there are some design problems of access and visibility, much of the difficulty derives from the general economic situation and competition from large scale retailers.

- *How do they compensate for the lack of usable open space?*
  EBALDC is attempting to get the use of an adjacent property for conversion to a teen recreation space. This would solve a significant part of the problem.

- *What is the impact of the project on the neighborhood?*
  The project has had a very positive impact on the neighborhood. It has transformed an underutilized, unattractive site into an attractive, vibrant, mixed use project, bringing life to the street, people to the neighborhood, and retail and social service opportunities. We were told that the "community is proud of it." Its theme of unity among diverse ethnic groups focuses the diversity of the neighborhood.

- *Were local contractors used?*
  The prime contractor is a local Danville firm who met or exceeded agreed-upon goals for hiring from the neighborhood and from among minority groups.

- *What is the quality of the design, image, appearance, and artwork?*
  Hismen Hin-Nu is one of the most attractive projects of its type and for its budget. It interprets a historically relevant local style (Mission Revival) and uses that design vocabulary to moderate its bulk and scale. The incorporation of culturally meaningful and diverse artworks enhances the appearance and is appreciated by residents and neighbors, who do perceive the place as being special.

- *What is the quality and durability of materials?*
  Materials and details are well chosen and executed. They are holding up well and can be expected to continue to do so, given the high quality of maintenance that is being provided.

- *Have any follow-up studies been done?*
  EBALDC has conducted a post construction assessment, focusing mainly on the process. They also appear to learn a considerable amount from prior projects and have a mechanism for ensuring that improvements are incorporated into subsequent ones.

- *What special resources were applied to the project (e.g., U.C. Berkeley or others) and how were they used; what did they contribute?*
  Students from University of California at Berkeley and University of Oregon, in a summer studio under the direction of the project architect, studied the site as part of an examination of a long stretch of East 14th Street, identifying it as having potential for dense, mixed use development.

Other Measures of Success

- *Leadership Effectiveness*
  EBALDC, together with their joint venture partner, San Antonio, provides an excellent example of an effective community developer. Well organized and apparently well managed, they have shown the ability to develop and operate projects like Hismen Hin-Nu and many others.

- *Prospects for Sustainability*
  There is every reason to believe that this project is sustainable financially and managerially, even though retail is struggling and not carrying its own weight. EBALDC has the financial strength to carry it, and the growing retail expertise to assist merchants with their operations.

- *Is This a Model Project?*
  While not unique for its medium to high density, this project is an excellent example of the successful integration of mixed uses (housing and commercial) along with on-site services. The quality of design is very high, with a very attractive image, appropriate and meaningful use of art, a good sense of open space and light, and a pattern of access and open space that encourages resident interaction. The process, while also not unique, was very strong, and included meaningful community participation resulting in real design decisions.

Selection Committee Comments

In the words of one Selection Committee member, this project "did a lot of things well." The Committee was particularly impressed with process and design; another Committee member asserted that "the process and the quality of the design are exemplary in comparison with other affordable housing." What the Committee liked so much about the process was the ways it found to include significant input from the community and from people like those who would live there. A relatively simple device, using modeling kits in a workshop setting, was viewed as a tremendous learning experience, both for the participants and the design professionals.

The theme of learning was echoed by the Committee's recognition of the fact that EBALDC actually follows up on its projects and, in an iterative process, tries to improve each one based on prior experience — it does not simply repeat a formula from the last project. "They're learning from this" was a committee member's observation. In addition, the collaboration between two community development corporations was viewed as an example of something that should happen more often and appears to have been very successful here, benefiting both organizations as well as the project.

The project's design was highly appreciated by the Committee, which found it unique and "stunning for the cost." Factors that were singled out included the appropriateness of the historical stylistic references (Mission style) to its local context and the generous and meaningful incorporation of art in the form of tiles, murals and the gate — which figured importantly in the project's name. The provision of larger apartments was found to be a proper response to the needs of residents and the Committee was impressed with the real ethnic mix, which they also found to be

Decorative street level exterior tile with African motif

positive, if somewhat unusual. However, given the level of understanding of, and sensitivity to, occupant requirements, the committee was a bit disappointed that the outdoor space needs of children had not been better anticipated and met.

There was a great deal of discussion about the difficulties being experienced by the retail outlets and, while the committee was very understanding of the problems posed by changes in the broader retail environment, they were also concerned about whether enough study of demand had been done and about certain aspects of the design — especially visibility. While recognizing that the project is located on a major retail thoroughfare, the committee commented that in many projects (not necessarily this one) there seems to be an over-reliance on retail in response to the need for economic development and, in many cases, other strategies and facilities (such as workshops, catering kitchens, light industry, or services) may be more appropriate. The committee noted that, if the project had received more conventional financing, lenders likely would have required a retail consultant who might have helped avoid or lessen the impact of some of the problems this project has experienced.

Finally, the committee was greatly impressed by EBALDC as an organization, representing what they saw as the best of a local nonprofit developer, with real ties in the community, an excellent relationship with the city, an evolving role in economic development, and strong, dynamic leadership. One Selection Committee member praised them by saying that EBALDC is "an organization that does what it does very well."

For More Information

East Bay Asian Local Development Corporation (EBALDC)
310–8th Street, Suite 200
Oakland, CA 94607

TEL: 510-287-5353

WEBSITE: www.ebaldc.com/organization/

silver MEDAL 1997

RUDY BRUNER AWARD
FOR URBAN EXCELLENCE

Center in the Square
Roanoke, Virginia

CENTER IN THE SQUARE

Center in the Square At A Glance

What is Center in the Square?

- A cultural center housing The Art Museum of Western Virginia; The Science Museum of Western Virginia; the Roanoke Valley Historical Museum; Mill Mountain Theatre; and the Arts Council of the Blue Ridge in one central location.[1]
- An organization that supports the arts and sciences through free rent for tenant organizations, marketing, and a variety of support services.
- The leading edge of the revitalization of the farmer's market/market area and downtown in Roanoke, Virginia.

Who Made the Submission?

- Center in the Square, a non-profit organization.

Major Goals of Center in the Square

- To provide support, including free rent and other services, for arts organizations so that they can focus their resources on programs and exhibits.
- To use arts and cultural activities to support education in Western Virginia schools.
- To provide for the adaptive reuse and preservation of an abandoned but historic building in the market area.
- To increase accessibility to the arts and sciences for Western Virginians and visitors.
- To provide a destination in downtown Roanoke to support market area revival.

Major Accomplishments of Center in the Square

- The arts organizations in Center in the Square are thriving, with numbers of visitors and quality of programs well beyond what would be expected in a city of its size.
- Center in the Square has become an important arts and sciences resource for the schools in Roanoke and Western Virginia.
- Center in the Square, and the organizations it supports, have become an important destination in Roanoke and an important draw for businesses and the city when they are marketing relocation to the area.
- The farmers' market is strong and is attracting a large and more diverse group of consumers.
- Downtown Roanoke, particularly in the area of the historic marketplace, has improved dramatically since the inception of Center in the Square. It is now a thriving destination for visitors and has a lively night life.

Reasons for Including Center in the Square as a Finalist

- Revival of the downtown is a critical issue in many small cities.

Center in the Square, including the McGuire Building and the Farmers Market

- Center in the Square emphasizes the importance of cultural organizations and programming in the civic life of urban centers.
- The initial planning process employed an innovative and effective mode of community participation.

Selection Committee Questions and Concerns for Site Visit

- How do the various entities and activities interact and coordinate? Is there cooperation, synergy, joint efforts? How often do visitors come to visit more than one cultural entity?
- What is the impact of Center in the Square on downtown and its immediate surroundings? Does the activity bring economic or other benefits to downtown? Are there traffic problems?
- How has it evolved or changed over the past 14 years? How has leadership succession been handled? Has leadership change led to changes in vision or programs?
- How well is the project linked to local schools and educational programs?
- How well does the architectural/interior design work? How has it been changed over time?

*Final Selection Committee Comments

- The Committee was impressed with the way Center in the Square used a broad, participatory process to reach out to the citizens of Roanoke in the initial planning stages.
- It was felt that more might have been done with the indoor and the outdoor space to further enhance the architecture of Center in the Square.
- Center in the Square has shown itself to be sustainable and has evolved since its inception.
- Center in the Square should continue to involve lower income and minority citizens in the management of the project.

Project Description

Project Chronology

1976 The Downtown Business League raises $100,000 to recruit business to downtown, and begins discussions that lead to Design '79.

Fall, 1976 Mill Mountain Theatre burns, creating impetus to search for alternative arts housing. Betty Carr Muse and George Cartledge Sr. first discuss concept of bringing all major arts organizations to one site.

1979 Design '79 is created to develop the downtown plan, rents a downtown storefront as its headquarters, and uses newspaper and television feedback sessions, and citizen workshops to produce report with recommendations and a catalog of design possibilities. One of the major recommendations is to provide a building downtown to serve as home for cultural organizations.

1978 The McGuire Building is identified as possible site by the Downtown Business League. Ezera Wertz buys a store to sell farm produce and John Williams opens Billy's Ritz restaurant, betting on revival of market area.

June 1979 McGuire Building accepted as site for cultural center. George Cartledge leases building for the group, and the Southwest Virginia Center for the Arts and Sciences, Inc. is chartered (its name is later changed to Western Virginia Foundation for Arts and Sciences).

February, 1981 Renovation work begins on the McGuire Building.

April, 1981 Center in the Square is formed as an operating entity for the foundation. Funding support from various sources reaches $5 million.

November, 1981 Groundbreaking for adjacent city garage, including space for theater and Planetarium.

July–August, 1982 Virginia General Assembly awards $2.6 million grant for construction of Center in the Square. $2.5 million tax-exempt bonds sold to complete financing.

December, 1983 Center in the Square holds official opening. 40,000 people participate in opening weekend.

1987 Phelps & Armistead Building, adjacent on Church Avenue, is purchased, adding 30,000 square feet to Center in the Square.

1989 $3 million renovation (50% private and 50% public funding) and expansion turns Phelps & Armistead Building into "Center on Church," with second theater, Arts Council office space, classrooms, workrooms, shops, etc.

May, 1990 Center on Church has gala opening.

1995 Hotel Roanoke reopens as refurbished hotel and conference center.

Key Participants *(persons interviewed are indicated by an asterisk*)*

Center in The Square
- James C. Sears, Ed. D.,* *President and General Manager, Center in the Square*
- Carolyn Nolan,* *Grants Officer*

City of Roanoke
- H. Bern Ewert,* *former City Manager*
- Dr. Noel Taylor,* *former Mayor*
- Bob Herbert,* *City Manager*
- Brian Wishneff,* *Brian Wishneff Associates (former Economic Development Coordinator)*

Downtown Business League *(all have been on Center Board of Directors)*
- John Hancock
- Frank Clement*
- George Cartledge Sr.
- Betty Carr Muse*
- Anne Hammersley
- Bill Hubard*

Center in the Square Board of Directors
- Warner Dalhouse,* *CEO, Dominion Bank (retired)*
- Dr. David Goode, *CEO, Norfolk Southern Corporation*
- Bittle Porterfield, III,* *Chairman*

Cultural Organizations
- Susan Jennings,* *The Arts Council of the Blue Ridge*
- Ken Schutz,* *The Science Museum of Western Virginia*
- Joanne Kuebler,* *The Art Museum of Western Virginia*
- Jere Hodgin,* *Mill Mountain Theatre*
- Rich Loveland,* *Roanoke Valley History Museum*

Downtown Business
- Sig Davidson,* *Davidsons*
- John Williams,* *Billy's Ritz*
- Richard Kurshan,* *Gessler Associates*

Farmers/Produce Sales
- Ezera Wertz*

Others
- Former State Senator William Hopkins*
- Claudia Whitworth,* *Publisher, Roanoke Tribune*

Architect
- Timm Jamieson,* *Hayes, Seay, Mattern & Mattern, Inc., Architects, Engineers, Planners*

Organization and Leadership

Center in the Square's mission is to:

> "Provide housing for cultural organizations in the Roanoke Valley… (as a) landlord; but a particularly beneficent landlord…By providing free space and absorbing the operating costs of that space…the Foundation frees the sponsored organizations from those mundane expenses (so that)…one hundred percent of each dollar raised by the organizations goes directly for the benefit of the community" (from "A Reinforcement and Expansion of the Basic Mission of Center in the Square," 1997).

The goal of Center has always been to assure the stability and viability of these organizations so that they can provide better quality arts and sciences "than should reasonably be expected in a community of this size." By putting all the organizations in one space, however, they also created a "critical mass (that) attracted public support, enthused the community and spawned economic benefits beyond anyone's wildest dream."

Center in the Square is a non-profit organization which maintains ownership of the physical facility and uses its facility, budget, staff and services to support "basic" arts and cultural organizations. The most important aspects of that support are rent-free space for five cultural organizations, providing them with maintenance, utilities, custodial services, security and various other services. The five organizations are:

- The Art Museum of Western Virginia
- The Science Museum of Western Virginia
- Roanoke Valley History Museum
- Mill Mountain Theatre
- The Arts Council of the Blue Ridge[1]

Center in the Square controls the building and its services, and its board has sole discretion over decisions of tenancy (that is, what new organizations might be added). The cultural organizations themselves are, however, totally independent in all internal decisions. They each have a board of directors which makes policy and personnel decisions. Each organization decides on its own programs and when, whether and how much to cooperate with other organizations. Joint programming between two organizations does not evolve from Center in the Square policy, but is decided by each player on judgments of mutual benefits, cost, timing, etc. The regular monthly meeting of the Center in the Square President and Executive Directors of all organizations is not to set policy or to make decisions to which all must adhere. Rather, it is a discussion and exchange of information among peers which can result in cooperation.

This loose structure evolved for both practical and philosophical reasons. When Center in the Square was created it was not clear that it could attract these, or any, important cultural organizations. Of over 50 invitation letters sent out, only these five responded positively. Organizers felt that serious organizations and competent directors would not be attracted if it meant giving up independence in making programming decisions.

In its 14 years of operation, through changes in its own directors and those of the member organizations, Center in the Square maintained continuity, and expanded its services in quality and outreach. Because cooperation is so largely based on the personal contacts among directors, each change "takes some getting used to," but the organization has demonstrated durability over time.

The Board of Directors is a primary source of stability and continuity. The original board was made up of the influential, civic minded and wealthy individuals who helped found Center in the Square. Several have remained members for the entirety of its existence. The board, concluding that it should have more turnover of membership, has instituted a three year term limit and has added members of the minority community to increase its diversity.

Project Context

The City and the Region

The City of Roanoke is located in a valley amid the Blue Ridge Mountains, in the lower part of the Shenandoah Valley. The valley served as a passage to the south, first for local Indian tribes and later for early American settlers. The barrier of the mountains limited early large scale development. Roanoke has always existed as a railroad town. The first trains came through in 1852, encouraging the development of tobacco warehouses and processing plants. The growth of the City of Roanoke can be traced to the junction there of east-west and north-south rail lines by the Norfolk and Western Railroad (N&W) in 1881. N&W set up their shops and operations in Roanoke and quickly began to buy and develop land for housing, maintenance facilities and offices. It built the Hotel Roanoke in 1882.

The downtown developed with a lively commercial area immediately adjacent to a marketplace, an area where farmers would sell their produce directly to consumers, largely in open air stalls. A market building was built in 1886 to house a meat market on the ground floor and an opera house upstairs.

19th century market scene at the McGuire Building

As Roanoke grew, it attracted a more diverse base of industry. As a transportation center and the largest city in the region it has served for more than a century as an economic and medical hub for the whole of southwestern Virginia and eastern West Virginia. As a symbol of its growth and pride, citizen groups erected an 88-foot wide illuminated star on Mill Mountain (overlooking the center of the city), touted as the largest man made star in United States. From this symbol the city took its nickname, "The Star City of the South."

After World War II, population and development spread outward from the city and into the county. Roanoke responded to population increases by annexing adjacent county land until the state legislature halted the practice in 1978. Since then there has been continued housing development of farm lands in Roanoke County and in other adjoining counties. The city's population is now approximately 100,000, with upwards of 250,000 living in the multi-county region. Roanoke classifies itself as "second tier city," and prides itself on the advantages of its lifestyle, such as low crime, slow pace, and moderate cost of living.

Center in the Square has garnered broad support in a state not known for arts funding, and a region in which jurisdictions have often been in conflict. Roanoke City and County, for example, have built separate jails and convention centers because of their difficulty working together. It is impressive that the city, the county, and other jurisdictions many miles away use, lay claim to, and provide financial backing for Center in the Square.

The Deterioration of Downtown

Many in Roanoke connect the decline of the downtown business district to the growth of shopping malls, which evolved from a few neighborhood centers in the 1960s to increasingly large regional malls in the 1970s and 1980s. Shoppers abandoned the downtown and stores fled to branches in the outlying malls as downtown vacancies mounted. As one Center in the Square director commented, "we were malled and Wal-Marted to death." Through the 70s the market area became home to adult book stores (6 at one count), "skid row-type bars," and prostitutes. Farmers in their open-air stalls remained, although fewer in number, and they saw business dwindle as many customers were afraid or unwilling to shop there. One farmer said the "good people would not come down."

John Williams was an early pioneer in re-establishing an upscale restaurant (Billy's Ritz) in the market area in 1979. Customers there would ask for window seats so that they could watch prostitutes as they strolled by to provide an ad hoc, but quite intentional floor show. There are also many stories that indicate a pervasive sense of pessimism among many that the deterioration of downtown and the trend towards the suburbs was irreversible. Civic leaders felt that a major effort was needed to improve the area or the farmers would leave and the market area would be abandoned.

Center in the Square —
Development and Implementation of the Idea

Center in the Square came from a "confluence of several events," says former Board President Warner Dalhouse. In 1976 a small group of business and civic leaders, who met regularly to discuss local matters, became alarmed at the state of deterioration of the downtown area and formed the Downtown Business League. Their purpose was to discuss ways of reviving the area. Over lunch, they collected $100,000 among themselves to start the process of recruiting businesses back to downtown.

In October of that year Mill Mountain Theatre burned down. Betty Carr Muse, daughter of League member John Hancock, and George Cartledge, also part of the businessmen's group, discussed possibilities for a replacement home for the theater. They came up with the idea of bringing several cultural organizations together at a downtown site. During this same period city officials, convinced that safe, convenient parking was critical for shoppers, were looking for ways to apply for Urban Development Action Grants (UDAG) to create a parking garage downtown.

Design '79 brought together these concerns, elements, and interests. Design '79 was a city-sponsored planning effort designed to seek community input and support for a plan to renew the market area as well as the broader downtown. A wide-scale effort was created to garner input. That effort included creating a storefront design center in the heart of downtown where passers-by could see and comment on plans that were posted in the window. The process was literally on display. Newspaper pieces presented ideas and solicited opinions. Most innovative (in this pre-talk radio era) was the use of a 3-hour prime time television design-a-thon to discuss renovation ideas and take on-air calls with viewer response. The final report of Design '79 called this "citizen participation on a scale never before attempted in the United States." Its stated goals were to "rekindle spirit," recreate the downtown as a "destination point," recycle older buildings, restore the historic market area, bolster retail sales, and develop vacant land.

Design '79 was guided by a steering committee of 15 prominent citizens and business leaders, several of whom were from the Downtown Business League, and the city manager.[2] It included citizen workshops with 50 community representatives. In the end over 3,000 ideas were received and over 1,000 of them used in the plan. For example, based on public input, the committee abandoned the idea of tearing down the library and developing that site along with the adjacent park. Instead, the library was expanded and the park re-landscaped.

The major recommendations of Design '79 included creating a bond issue to finance capital improvements in the downtown/market area, exploring the feasibility of creating a hotel-convention center complex downtown, and developing a cultural center to bring together several cultural organizations to downtown.

While there was some support for clearing out the farmer's stalls, the final plan kept the farmer's market as the centerpiece of the revitalization.

Obtaining a facility involved both the very public planning process and the private discussions of Business League members. While Design '79 recommended putting a cultural center downtown, it did not suggest a site. Several had been mentioned including the library and post office buildings. A consultant, however, suggested putting the center in the market area, to play upon and reinforce the natural strengths of the farmers market. When Business League members learned in 1979 of the availability of the McGuire Building, an abandoned farm implements warehouse in the center of the market area, Cartledge personally leased the building to hold it as a possible site. Later that year it was purchased from the owner and officially adopted for the cultural center.

Turning Center in the Square into a reality involved finding the funding to complete the restoration of the site, and convincing the cultural organizations to become tenants. Even though private fundraising went well, banks were not willing to lend construction funds on such pledges. When it was clear that state funds would be needed, Senator William Hopkins was recruited. Hopkins was the legislator from the area and majority leader in the state senate. Although Hopkins was successful in getting his friends in the legislature to appropriate funds for the idea, the price tag continued to rise. The eventual cost of the heating, ventilation, and air conditioning systems alone exceeded the original estimate for the construction, requiring several additional requests for an increased level of funding. Eventually (after hiring a train to bring the governor and entire legislature to Roanoke to be wined, dined and regaled with city plans and funding requests) Center in the Square received $2.6 million from the state for construction, which, along with bonds and private contributions allowed construction to begin.

Only five cultural organizations expressed serious interest in joining this new venture. Mill Mountain Theatre and the Arts Council were obvious candidates — neither had a permanent home. The Science Museum was in a small school house with an uninspiring collection ("a lot of things in pickle jars"). The Historical Society had a small store front collection in an out-of-the-way area. The Art Museum was in the best shape. It had use of a stately old home in the posh section of Roanoke, where most of its board and patrons lived. The Art Museum was particularly concerned about moving downtown, away from its base and to a place where its patrons were reluctant to travel, even though they might have only a few dozen visitors in a weekend. The Art Museum eventually came — as did the other four organizations — although it was said to have arrived "kicking and screaming," enticed by an offer its board could not refuse — free rent.

There is some disagreement about the role of the city in developing Center in the Square. Some people who were involved at the early stages feel that the city was not sufficiently active in promoting the project, in terms of obtaining funding or promoting public

Design '79 community meeting

support. They suggest that the city was largely interested in Urban Development Action Grant (UDAG) funding and was on the sidelines for much of the early struggle. Hopkins said that the city council wanted no part of the project, which they saw as driven by the "silk stocking crowd" - not their prime constituency.

Others, including city officials, place city government more squarely in the middle of the process. Dr. Noel Taylor, mayor at the time, is quite passionate in saying that the creation of Center in the Square was a joint effort of government, business, and the community. Current city officials indicate that public opinion would not have supported direct city spending for downtown revival. Downtown was seen as too unlikely a candidate for success. Rather, they suggest, the city manager had to act "covertly," supporting the process without risking public exposure that could have threatened the entire effort. They point to the street improvements in the market area as evidence of city action. John Williams notes that his partners took the risk of investing in their early upscale restaurant based on assurances from the city manager that the downtown would be revived.

Current Status and Impact on Organizations

Center in the Square was, by all accounts, an instant hit with citizens as well as the tenant organizations. Forty thousand people came for the opening weekend. Billy's Ritz saw business increase immediately by fifty percent. The Art Museum had more visitors in its first three weeks than it had drawn in any of the previous five years. Moreover, the crowd of visitors was much more diverse. One informant saw an African-American family, formally dressed on a Sunday afternoon, touring the Art Museum during the opening weekend. He had never recalled seeing an African-American visitor in the former location. "It was then that I knew we had done something special."

Overall, attendance at the tenant organizations has increased from six to twenty fold since the opening of Center in the Square. The Art Museum had 10,000 visitors in 1983, compared to 84,000 visitors in 1996. The Science Museum's audience increased from 11,000 to 197,000, and the History Museum and Theatre went from 8,000 and 6,400 visitors respectively to 34,400 and 71,500 visitors[3].

The organizations have also grown in sophistication of programs. Center in the Square helps in this respect in several ways. First, directors are able to focus their attention and fundraising on programs and exhibits, not rent and maintenance. Second, there is an expanded audience, in number and diversity, which increases the demand for improved and expanded program content. Third, there are opportunities for synergistic cooperation among the organizations. All of these organizations do indeed offer programs that are of a higher quality than one would expect in a city of this size.

For example, Mill Mountain Theatre offers a broad variety of high quality productions for adults and children, with an emphasis on new works. The Science Museum has a large and sophisti-

Opening of Center in the Square

cated set of exhibits and will soon see its weather center become the locale for regular television weather report broadcasts. The Art Museum's collection has several small but selective areas of excellence. The History Museum has grown from a few artifacts in a store-front to a variety of exhibits, including hands-on archeological experiences.

Interaction and coordination among the member organizations is purely voluntary, although it is enhanced by proximity and the collegiality of monthly executive director meetings. Several people noted that they interact somewhat less now than in the recent past because of stresses caused by cuts in government funding for the arts. The Executive Directors say that they spend much more of their time on basic administration and program development and haven't been able to afford the time or staff for major coordination of efforts. There are, however, several significant examples of synergies, such as the summer camp program that includes use of most of the facilities.

Occasionally organizations collaborate on a specific program (such as when the Art Museum arranged a Seurat exhibit coincident with the opening of "Sunday in Park with George" at the theater). Through the aegis of Center in the Square, they engage in joint marketing and special events. There are no good data on the rate of individual versus multi-site visits.

The process of inventing Center in the Square shows an interesting interplay of public and private processes. Much of the early leadership, planning and critical ideas came from a private group of civic-minded businessmen, who knew and in some ways shaped the city. These same people, however, opened the process through Design '79 as Roanoke ran an extraordinarily public and inclusive effort that proactively sought input from the entire populace. The Downtown Business League was responsible for much of the energy, ideas, and private funding that made the Center in the Square happen and for years made up much of the board of directors. Center in the Square has recently sought to

Mill Mountain Theatre with small stage

Local Colors, an annual multi-cultural event

expand and diversify its boards, leading to much of the recent change at the board level.

Nevertheless, there is a question about the degree to which Center in the Square is "owned" by all its citizens. Some leaders in the African-American community, while being strong supporters of Center in the Square, argue that they have not been, and are not yet, fully involved in the planning of programs and events. The Center is still seen as something done by the city for them, rather than by them. Dr. Noel Taylor, on the other hand, an African-American who was mayor for 17 years, strongly feels that Center in the Square represents the whole citizenry of the area. Center in the Square has begun to diversify (three minority members were recently added to the board) and focused more resources on "Local Colors," a Market Square ethnic celebration.

Impact on the Market, Downtown and the Region

While there have been dramatic improvements in the market area, it would be unfair to suggest that Center in the Square was the sole or direct cause of all of these changes. Rather, Center in the Square was the leading edge of a wave of changes, and its considerable success made each of the improvements that followed both easier and more likely to succeed. These include thirteen new and mostly upscale restaurants, the rehabilitation and adaptive reuse of the old market building into a food court, and a variety of new retail stores, including an Orvis store. The many restaurants in the compact area of the market, some with live music, create a busy, lively and distinctly urban street presence during the day and evenings.

Many of the other Design '79 recommendations have been carried out. The library has been expanded and its adjacent park re-landscaped, and a number of new office buildings have been added to the downtown area, including a 21 story bank tower. While not architecturally distinguished, its visible presence on the skyline is symbolic of Roanoke's economic strength and downtown revival.

Also significant was the recent re-opening of the Hotel Roanoke. The hotel had been owned and run by the Norfolk and Western for over 100 years, but declined as the railroad reduced its presence in Roanoke. It finally closed in 1990. The grand scale of the hotel is hard to miss on entering downtown and its closing was very distressing, symbolizing the loss of something special. It was renovated with public and private investment, and reopened as a hotel/convention center in partnership with Virginia Polytechnic Institute, thirty miles away in Blacksburg. Public funding contributed $7 million to a glass-enclosed bridge over the rail tracks that for the first time makes the hotel a part of the downtown. While Center in the Square was not directly responsible for the hotel's revival, it is an important destination for hotel guests. The strength of the market area played an important role in making the $40+ million renovation possible.

The improvements to downtown are not complete. There remain struggling businesses in the market area and vacancies a

John Williams at his store located in the basement of CITS

few blocks away. Downtown lost its last department store recently[4]. On the other hand, about a mile north of Center in the Square an old high school has been converted by the city into the Jefferson Center, housing a variety of civic and cultural functions (one Center board member commented "they got our overflow"). The Jefferson Center differs from Center in the Square in many ways (including different funding sources and kinds of organizations) but city officials say that the success of Center in the Square made the Jefferson Center easier to promote and carry forward.

All of the facilities in Center in the Square have strong educational components, and several have children as a significant portion of their visitors. It is a regional resource, drawing visitors from as far as an hour and a half drive away. Schools throughout the area regularly bring classes there, with the Science Museum as the most popular attraction. The museums are formally presented as curriculum options in materials available to teachers in Roanoke city and county. School administrators, teachers and parents with whom we spoke make it clear that Center in the Square is an important element in the art and science education of children in the region.

Center in the Square also plays a role in local economic development plans. In addition to the direct benefits of a growing downtown and market area, several local and Center in the Square officials stressed the importance of cultural offerings to business executives mulling Roanoke as one of several possibilities for relocation.

Glass enclosed bridge connects Hotel Roanoke to the downtown.

Young visitors at the Science Museum of Western Virginia

Design and Maintenance

Center in the Square is a combination of an adaptive reuse of the McGuire Building, a large, white brick, 5-story L-shaped building with walls and columns designed to bear heavy loads, and a new, attached facility with a 320 car garage and space for a planetarium and theater. The building's historic character is considerably enhanced with restoration of its original cornice, completed in 1997.

One enters into a 5-story atrium where the addition joins the historic structure, with a circular staircase that has a landing at the entrance of each of the museums. The large and somewhat obtrusive white metal railings have a beveled top to reduce the risk of children climbing and falling. The railings run along the entire length of the stairway and suggest to some the homey qualities of picket fences. Each floor of the garage has a direct enclosed entrance to the corresponding museum floor. It was designed for easy access without steps, with elderly art patrons in mind. The architect notes that they were concerned originally about having too large an empty space in the first floor entry, but it is apparent now that they underestimated demand, leaving the lobby crowded and circulation difficult on some days.

The facility includes
- A three tier 407-seat main space for Mill Mountain Theatre;
- A 125-seat "black box" stage for experimental theater productions;
- The Art Museum of Western Virginia (28,000 square feet);
- The Science Museum of Western Virginia with almost 37,000 square feet of space and the 125 seat William B. Hopkins Planetarium;
- Roanoke Valley History Museum (17,000 square feet);
- Offices for The Arts Council of the Blue Ridge;
- 3 museums stores on the ground floor;
- Retail space (including the Roanoke Weiner stand, a local institution that predates Center in the Square, and Orvis, a store in the national chain);
- Indoor retail space for produce vendors, contiguous to the outdoor stalls, which are owned and controlled by the city. Center in the Square rents space to produce vendors at reduced rates to support the market.

The addition on Church Avenue, in the back of the original building, has significantly added to the amount and quality of space, although it has created some awkward connections. The Art

Central staircase in Center's atrium

Museum, in particular, has a space that traverses both buildings with some labyrinthian passageways.

Center management plans some changes to the building's external appearance in the coming year, in addition to the cornice replacement. In particular, they are concerned that their banners are hidden from view of pedestrians by the awnings on the Orvis storefront. They will replace the banners, and other signs which they say were too conservative in the original plan, with larger and more striking ones.

Development Costs

McGuire Building

Purchase McGuire Building	$250,000
Purchase land for garage	$132,000
Foundation for parking	$942,512
Garage Construction (incl. 2nd Theater & Planetarium)	$6,874,640
Subtotal	*$8,199,152*

Phelps & Armistead Building (Center On Church)

Purchase	$200,000
Construction	$3,084,764
Subtotal	*$3,284,764*
Total	**$11, 483,916**

Sources

McGuire Building (Center in the Square)

Pledges	$4,000,000
State Grant	$2,600,000
Bank Consortium	$2,500,000
Subtotal	*$9,100,000*

Phelps & Armistead Building (Center on Church)

Donations	$1,500,000
State Grant	$1,500,000
Subtotal	*$3,000,000*
Grand Total	**$12,100,000**

Operating Budget

INCOME		EXPENSES	
Grants		Salaries	$414,432
State	$461,915	Benefits	$110,287
City of Roanoke	$150,000	Travel	$4,030
County of Roanoke	$55,000	Contractual Services*	$331,908
City of Salem	$10,000	Marketing & Advertising	$69,882
Botetourt County	$5,000	Public Relations	$14,755
Franklin County	$5,000	Volunteers	$3,300
Bedford County	$5,000	Supplies	$43,145
Contributions	$320,000	Development	
Investment Income	$120,651	Annual Campaign	$59,386
Rentals	$38,969	Endowment Campaign	$173,189
Other Income	$2,200	**Total Expenses**	**$1,224,314**
(phone commission, tours, etc.)			
Special Events, Misc.	$55,000		

Total Income $1,228,735
Net Inc./Loss from Operations $4,421
Depreciation $335,100
Net Income/Loss **($330,679)**

* includes utilities, phone, security, custodial, insurance, etc.

Display at Roanoke Valley Historical Museum

Finances

Development

Center in the Square was able to cover purchase and construction costs without need of a mortgage, so that yearly operating expenses could be met without charging the tenants rent. The City of Roanoke contributed to the project's development costs primarily through the application of UDAG funds for the parking structure.

Operations

The largest portion of the operating income — almost $700,000 — comes from the contributions made by various governmental agencies. These funds include large contributions from the state, city, and county, as well as smaller amounts from neighboring jurisdictions. The fact that so many jurisdictions contribute shows the value they place in the Center. This support is largely in recognition of the benefits for local schools.

Not in the budget is the almost $1.7 million of uncollected rent and services from the tenant organizations. The Art Museum, for example, lists in its annual report "donated premises" valued at $357,510, out of a total budget of $1.1 million. The value for the other organizations of the donated rent is also approximately one-third of their annual budget.

Current Projects and Future Plans

The management of Center in the Square has a number of plans for growth to support cultural institutions in Roanoke. In the near term they expect to expand beyond its current site. A purchase agreement was recently signed on a historic downtown hotel just one block from the current facility. After significant renovation, this hotel will serve as a dormitory for Mill Mountain Theatre actors, will house a children's drama enrichment program, and will provide significant retail space on the first of its three floors.

Planning is also underway for the construction of an 80,000 square foot addition to Center in the Square that will house new facilities for the Art Museum and for Mill Mountain Theatre.

Two more organizations have recently been added to the Center's family — the ballet and the opera companies. Both represent what Center in the Square sees as basic cultural institutions, and are in need of support to maintain their viability. Since space in the complex is limited, Center in the Square pays the rental fees that the ballet and opera companies incur at their current homes, giving them most of the same financial support as its other tenants, although they don't have the benefit of a central location.

Center in the Square has also begun to raise funds for an endowment, which would provide a cushion should public arts funding be reduced in the future. They have pledges for about 25% of their $12 million goal, and are confident of achieving the rest in the next few years.

Center in the Square and each of its individual organizations have a variety of plans for programmatic expansion, including adding to public activities at the Market Square (such as the Local Colors ethnic festival we attended), and increasing contacts with school districts.

Assessing Project Success

How Well is Center in the Square Meeting its Goals?

- *To provide support, including free rent and other services, for arts organizations so that they can concentrate on programs and exhibits.*

  Center in the Square is meeting this goal well. The Center and its tenant organizations are on sound financial footing.

- *Adaptive reuse and preservation of an abandoned but historic building.*

Center in the Square has done a good job creating a functional and well used space out of a warehouse building. There are some design concerns particularly in circulation space and signage (the latter is being addressed in current plans).

- *Easy accessibility to the arts for citizens and visitors.*
The most easily quantifiable success of Center in the Square is the multi-fold increase in attendance by all of its tenant organizations. The arts in Roanoke and its surrounding region are of better quality, more easily reached, far better used, and visited by a broader and more diverse audience. Center in the Square has recently added minority board members, but still needs to increase its outreach to the minority community.

Response to Selection Committee Questions and Concerns

- *How do the various entities and activities interact and coordinate? Is there cooperation, synergy, joint efforts? How often do visitors come to visit just one versus several?*
There are examples of cooperation and synergy from having these organizations together, but these are not the main reason for their coming to the Center in the Square, and do not represent a large part of their programming.

- *What is the impact of Center in the Square on downtown and its immediate surroundings. Does the activity bring economic or other benefits to downtown? Are there traffic problems?*
Center in the Square has had a major impact on the revival of the market area and downtown. It cannot be credited with sole responsibility for the improvements, but it was called the lynchpin effort and one of first in series of related changes leading to the turnaround of the area. Center in the Square has also been credited with helping to attract companies relocating to the area. Streets in the area get congested occasionally, but traffic problems are not overwhelming.

Entrance to Center in the Square

- *How has it evolved or changed over the past 14 years? How has leadership succession been handled? Has leadership change led to changes in vision or programs?*

  Center in the Square has continuously grown, both programmatically and physically. It has expanded into new buildings and the tenant organizations have grown in the size and ambition of their programs. They have a number of plans for future expansion. Through several changes of directors, Center in the Square has come to recognize that fundraising and public relations are the two most critical aspects of the position.

- *How well is the project linked to local schools and educational programs?*

  Center in the Square has become an integral part of the school programs for Roanoke City, Roanoke County and many more distant schools. The Science Museum and Art Museum, in particular, have become important supplements for school programs. The largest number of visitors are children in organized groups.

Farmer's market at Center in the Square

- *How well does the architectural/interior design work? How has it been changed over time?*

  Center in the Square is not groundbreaking or exciting architecturally but the design works for its purpose. The interior court, while too small, provides good visual access to all areas and floors (although signage needs upgrading and the entry to the theater is hard to identify). The facility offers good access to the garage.

Impact on the Neighborhood

As noted above, the impact on the neighborhood has been positive and significant in scope. The most immediate and significant effect seems limited to the three or four block area around the marketplace. The downtown area beyond that has shown signs of improvement, although there are still a number of vacancies. There have been improvements at the other end of downtown (the Jefferson Center) and one goal is to fill in development between these two anchors.

Quality of the Physical Place

Center in the Square is an open and inviting cultural center that is very well used (especially by school children), and is located in the midst of a now-thriving and bustling market area. It is an important cultural, entertainment, and tourist destination in Roanoke. The marketplace area has been transformed from a dying and deteriorating place to one of restaurants, music, retail and a vibrant day and night street life. The mix of farm stands, restaurants, retail and museums/theaters in a very compact space has created a significant urban attraction for Roanoke.

Values

- Center in the Square is a statement that the arts are a basic and important element of community life, not an expendable luxury.
- Preservation played a role in this project. This was not just by maintaining and restoring the McGuire Building, certainly

not the most interesting structure in the area, but in the preservation and invigoration of the farmers' market and the market area.

- Center in the Square also represents a significant democratization of the arts. As a southern city, Roanoke was institutionally segregated until the 1960s. The cultural institutions were clearly the province of the white establishment — by location and patronage. Because of their current location downtown and their outreach to the schools, these art and science organizations have more fully reached the diverse population of the region.

Sustainability and Replicability

Center in the Square is 14 years old, and has shown that it can sustain itself over time and through periods of cutbacks in arts funding. Officials have difficulty imagining a situation that could force them to ask tenant organizations for rent. It has announced a $12 million endowment campaign as a hedge against future cutbacks in government funding.

Market stalls adjacent to McGuire Building

The revival of downtown Roanoke has not gone unnoticed by other "2nd tier cities," many of whom have similar problems. Many have sent officials to visit and several (including Buffalo, New York and Charleston, West Virginia) have initiated more formal attempts to study or model Center in the Square. Asheville, North Carolina developed a downtown cultural center based, in a significant part, on Center in the Square, although it is not nearly as successful.

Selection Committee Comments

The Selection Committee was impressed at the way Center in the Square made use of a broad and participatory process to reach out to the citizens of Roanoke for help in the initial planning stages. They appreciated the scale of the effort to bring arts to downtown Roanoke as a way to improve the quality of, and access to, these crucial amenities, as well as to support the redevelopment of the area.

The Selection Committee was somewhat critical of the aesthetic quality of the design, feeling that more might have been done with the indoor and outdoor space to enhance the area. They also noted that, while the facility has served the whole community in many important ways, lower income and minority citizens were not a significant part of the early planning process, and remain under represented on the board of directors, despite the fact that steps are being taken to address this concern.

All in all, the Selection Committee felt that Center in the Square has shown itself to be sustainable, and has evolved and improved since its inception. It continues to increase then number of arts organizations under its umbrella, and actively seeks ways to reach more people (usually children) with the arts and sciences. It has had a significant positive impact on the revival of the market area and downtown Roanoke.

Endnotes

1. (On July 1, 1997, the Western Virginia Foundation for the Arts and Sciences, operating as Center in the Square added two organizations to its family — Opera Roanoke and Roanoke Ballet Theatre, Inc., making a total of seven beneficiary organizations. The two additional organizations are located in the Jefferson Center.)

2. Design '79 was funded 40% by the Downtown Business League and 60% by the city.

3. These figures include all visitors served, including programs taken off-site, such as to schools.

4. City officials argue that this loss was part of a larger trend and that the Center in the Square presence delayed the closing. There are several plans for the reuse of this large facility.

References

Blueprint 2000: A Vision for the Cultural Community of the Roanoke Region of Western Virginia: final Report and Recommendations.

The Arts Council of the Blue Ridge, 1992.

Roanoke Design '79, City of Roanoke, 1979.

White, Clare. Roanoke: 1740-1982, Roanoke Valley Historical Society, 1982.

For More Information

Center in the Square
One Market Square
Roanoke, VA 24011

TEL: 540-342-5708

WEBSITE: www.cits.org

silver MEDAL 1997

RUDY BRUNER AWARD
FOR URBAN EXCELLENCE

Cleveland Historic Warehouse
Cleveland, Ohio

HISTORIC WAREHOUSE DISTRICT

The Cleveland Historic Warehouse District at a Glance

What is the Cleveland Historic Warehouse District?

- Adaptive reuse of a significant number of vacant historic commercial buildings on the edge of downtown Cleveland to residential, office, and retail uses.

Who Made the Submission?

- The Historic Warehouse District Development Corporation of Cleveland (HWDDC).

Major Goals

- Reversal of the wholesale demolition of historic warehouses, a process which had taken place in the district in response to demand for surface parking created by the City/County Justice Center and State Office Building located nearby.
- Establishment of mechanisms to protect and rehabilitate the historic warehouse buildings.
- Creation of a mixed use residential neighborhood with a critical mass of at least 1,500 residents in the heart of downtown.
- Attracting middle class people back to the city which had become predominately lower income.
- Clean up of blight caused by a concentration of under-utilized warehouse buildings.

Reasons for Including the Warehouse District as a Finalist

- Importance of bringing back middle class residents to the city.
- Enlightened use of building codes and financing mechanisms.
- Importance of preserving structures of historic value in the downtown.

Selection Committee Questions and Concerns for Site Visit

- Who was the motivating force for the project? Is there a strong leading entity? What is the project's current constituency and level of support?
- Has the area come together as a whole district or neighborhood yet? Is enough done; has it achieved critical mass?
- Are there significant pieces that are not yet done (buildings not renovated, vacant land, infrastructure not complete)? If so, does this contribute to a feeling of being unfinished? For elements that are not finished are there real plans, timetables and financing for their completion?
- What are vacancy rates for residential and commercial?
- Is the area lively? Are there people on the streets? At what times of day or week? Were there artists or other marginal users living

The Warehouse District is located on the bluffs overlooking the Cuyahoga River.

there before the project (even illegally)? If so, what happened to them; are they still there?
- Has the district had an impact on the surrounding area and on the balance of downtown?
- Has mid-level governance evolved (neighborhood association, etc.)? Are services provided? Are they adequate?
- What is the design quality of the original structures and the renovations?

Final Selection Committee Comments
- The Committee commended the Historic Warehouse District on the preservation of an important group of historic structures, and on introducing residential and new commercial uses into the downtown.
- The Committee felt that the district has yet to realize its potential in terms of coherent vision, urban impact, and quality of design. Much of its character and impact will depend upon the future disposition of the large unfinished areas in the heart of the district.
- There was some concern that while the City is now playing an active and supportive role with respect to the Historic Warehouse District, the City, in a period of crisis, shared responsibility for the initial deterioration of the fabric of the neighborhood.

Project Description

Chronology

Mid–1800s to early 1900s Evolution of the district into a major warehouse and manufacturing zone based on its location on the bluffs where the Cuyahoga River joins Lake Erie.

1960–1970s Over half of the historic structures in the area torn down for surface parking lots.

Late 1979 Protests stop threatened demolition of the Hilliard Block, oldest building in area.

1980 Formation of Historic Warehouse District Development Corporation of Cleveland.

1982 Designation of National Historic District; Hilliard block becomes a landmark.

1985 Initiation of master planning for the Historic District.

1991 Adoption of Historic Warehouse District Master Plan into Civic Vision, the city-wide Master Plan.

1991–1996 Investment in 30 buildings (new and historic) with a total of $125 million in private and public funds, for 1,000 residents, office space, and retail and commercial uses.

Key Participants *(persons interviewed are indicated by an asterisk*)*

Historic Warehouse District Development Corporation of Cleveland
Katherine Boruff,* *Executive Director*
Jonathan Sandvick,* *Chairman of the Board of Directors*
Bill Boyer,* *Board of Directors*
Marilyn Casey,* *Board of Directors*
Bill Gould,* *Board of Directors*
Mike Miller, *Board of Directors*
Vic Pascucci, *Board of Directors*
Richard Sheehan, *Board of Directors*

City of Cleveland
Hunter Morrison,* *Director of Planning*
Terri D. Hamilton,* *Director of Community Development*
Paul Krutko,* *Downtown Housing Manager*
Steven Seaton,* *Manager of Business Retention/Expansion, Department of Economic Development*

Community Groups
Ken Stapleton,* *Downtown Development Coordinator*
Kathy Coakley,* *Committee for Public Art*

Anda Cook,* *Living in Cleveland*
Tom Yablonsky,* *Historic Gateway Neighborhood Development Corp.*
Steve Strnisha,* *Deputy Director, Cleveland Tomorrow Inc.*

Foundations
   The Chilcote Foundation,* Lee Chilcote *(also board member of HWDDC)*
   The Cleveland Foundation, Jay Talbot,* *Senior Program Officer*
   The Murphy Foundation, Allan J. Zambie,* *Vice President*
   The Gund Foundation

National City Bank
   Jim Evans*

Developers
   Randy Alexander (National Terminals),* *The Alexander Co., Madison, Wisconsin*
   Ric Hammitt (Bradley Building)*
   Neil Viny (Hat Factory; Hoyt Block),* *The Deland Group*
   Dave Gruenewald (Worthington/URS; 425 Lakeside),* *Jacobs Investments*
   Bob Rains (seven projects),* *Landmark Properties*

Development of the Warehouse District
(This section relies on sources provided by the HWDDC, including their walking tour brochure and draft revised Master Plan of 1997.)

The Warehouse District occupies a strategic location on the bluffs above the Cuyahoga River where it flows into Lake Erie. The town's first settlement was here, since the lower lying land closer to the waterways was too marshy and insect-infested to provide appropriate building sites. While housing was built first, by the middle of the Nineteenth Century it was replaced with more intense uses as the district became the city's financial and business center. The warehouses housed large hardware distributors, marine suppliers and garment manufacturers. Smaller businesses included dry goods, grocers, tool suppliers, and ship's chandlers. Larger office buildings served as headquarters for the iron, coal, and shipping industries. The garment industry gradually expanded so that by the 1920s Cleveland ranked close to New York City as a leading center of clothing manufacture. There were also hotels and saloons in the area, as well as the city's newspaper offices and a theater which was the site of John Wilkes Booth's last performance prior to his assassination of Lincoln.

Many of the existing buildings date from the middle and later nineteenth century, while some are more recent. The earlier structures are built of heavy timber with brick exteriors, though the finer buildings are clad, at least partly, in stone. Later buildings began to take advantage of new construction techniques, such as cast iron columns which allowed a more open facade with larger glass areas. Still later structures were built of reinforced concrete, but generally still clad in brick. Some of the warehouses have fewer and smaller windows than the manufacturing buildings which have larger glass areas needed to provide natural illumina-

Warehouse District in foreground with Society Tower beyond

tion for the tasks being performed. Most have high ceilings, allowing easy conversion into loft apartments and open offices.

Decline of the District and the Move for Preservation

After World War II, the district started to suffer serious decline as manufacturers began to abandon the area. This accelerated in the early 1970s, when the remaining large wholesale/retail occupant, the Worthington Company, moved out of the district. Buildings were increasingly abandoned and, at that time, the City placed little value on the historic structures — allowing them to be demolished and replaced by surface parking lots, then considered the "highest and best use." The demand for parking was, in fact, stimulated by city and county actions, including construction of a large justice center with inadequate parking. More than half of the historic structures in the district were destroyed at this time. There were very few people living in the district, mostly urban pioneers and artists, some of whom were living illegally in their studios. Many buildings were vacant and a large pornography shop occupied a building that today houses an upscale Italian restaurant.

Perry-Payne Building in the late 19th Century

Warehouse District, mid-19th century

The critical moment and turning point for the district came in 1979, with an event that made people more acutely aware that the city was losing its history and heritage — and could do something about it. Protests by preservationists stopped demolition of the Hilliard Building, dating from 1849, the district's oldest remaining structure. This successful protest led more or less directly to the formation of the Historic Warehouse District Development Corporation in 1980, its initiation of a survey of the historic structures, and the successful effort to get the district listed on the National Register of Historic Places, and on the Cleveland Landmark List, in 1982. This series of actions effectively stopped the demolition of historic structures in the district.

The Historic Warehouse District Development Corporation

The Historic Warehouse District Development Corporation (HWDDC) has four main roles and responsibilities: it maintains an inventory of the buildings in the district, performs design review, offers marketing services for the district, and provides development teams and building owners with assistance in obtaining project approvals and financing. Design review is a mandatory step with HWDDC approval required by the City before it will proceed with a project. The review is based on detailed, clearly articulated guidelines which are intended to be consistent with other review agencies and, thus, to help applicants progress more easily through those later reviews. In addition to its regular activities, HWDDC also provided assistance in changing the state building code to give greater flexibility for the rehabilitation of historic buildings.

In terms of its organization and leadership, HWDDC has a group of very active trustees who are involved both in ongoing activities and in giving direction to initiatives (see What is Planned, below). HWDDC also has over 100 active volunteers as well as broad community support through membership, donations, and patronage of fundraising events. HWDDC's 1995 annual budget was about $275,000, of which about $175,000 came from grants and donations with the balance mostly generated by fundraising events.

HWDDC is one of approximately 30 local development corporations in Cleveland. The City and the organization itself view HWDDC as the "premier non-profit organization in downtown for preservation and redevelopment" and perceive the Warehouse District as pioneering the movement to bring residents back to the downtown area. As the district demonstrated that downtown could be attractive, adjacent areas such as Gateway have begun to convert older buildings to rental housing. In addition, there are at least two examples of innovative programs for which HWDDC is seen as pioneering for the rest of the city. One is the creation of one of the City's first Special Improvement Districts (SID) and the other is the creation of historic conservation easements, both of which were in process during the site visit and were expected to be emulated by others (see section below on What is Planned).

Signifigant historic buildings were demolished to provide surface parking.

What Has Been Done

The Historic Warehouse District covers nine square blocks which comprise 43 acres. Since 1982, and especially since 1991, a great deal has been accomplished in the district. Residential projects which have been completed or are in process of construction in 1997 include the following number of housing units:

Status	Units	Estimated Residents
Occupied (as of early 1997)	624	936
To be completed in 1997	354	531
Total	**978**	**1,467**

In addition, significant amounts of office space have been created through renovation of historic buildings. Many commercial and retail spaces have also been added, including many restaurants, bars and clubs. In total, over two and one-half million square feet have been renovated. New construction has included additions and a few new buildings. Overall, more than half of the space in the district has been renovated, with a few large and difficult buildings on the edge of the zone accounting for much of the non-renovated space.

Street improvements have been completed in a few areas, but they are limited to only a portion of the paved area between the building and the street. A few areas have historic lighting fixtures with the remainder of the districts to be done by the city-owned electric company. The city now requires individual building owners to complete the street improvements as they renovate buildings, but those who renovated in the 1980s did not do the improvements.

Several art projects have been completed in the district by the Committee for Public Art, which has been active there for many years. Examples include:

- **West Sixth Streetscape** A national open competition with over 300 entries led to the selection of Seattle artist Lewis "Buster" Simpson. Inspired by the district's history of warehousing — with crates stacked on the sidewalks — he created stacks of sandstone blocks as seating/sculpture and also proposed sandstone and brick pavers on the sidewalks. Crafted between 1985 and 1988, these installations are still in place.
- **"Art Behind Bars"** consisted of installations behind the security bars in some windows of an old warehouse at street level on an active thoroughfare connecting the Warehouse District to the flats. Forty artists contributed to 24 month-long installations from 1986 to 1988.
- **"Signs of Life"** fostered collaborations between artists and businesses to create inventive and expressive street signs for a number of shops. Created from 1987 to 1988, most of the signs have disappeared.

What Is Planned

The current emphasis for the district — apparently shared by all relevant agencies and organizations — is on housing, especially housing for sale. The goal is to add to the diversity of the neighborhood by attracting stable residents who will have a continuing stake in the area — in other words, middle class households — a group that abandoned the city for the suburbs. Diversity will also be added at the other end of the spectrum through the inclusion of more than 120 low/moderate income units in the National Terminals and Water Street Apartment projects; see case study below. At the time

Granite blocks symbolizing packing crates, and decorative paving on West Sixth Street

of writing, the for-sale market was about to be tested in a small way by a six unit project being developed by the HWDDC (see the case study on Kirkham Place). It appears that other developers are now planning housing for sale, initially as condo conversions of warehouse space.

Most of the best and more promising buildings have been or are being renovated. Only a few of the remaining buildings will be easy candidates for renovation, and most of them are being held by investors in hopes that the market will strengthen and they will be able to sell them at a profit. On the other hand, the higher prices they will command will make them more difficult to bring on line within market rents. The "problem" and difficult properties — those that are poorly located or configured, or have significant contamination or structural problems — may languish unimproved for a considerable time into the future. In fact, as the Warehouse District has become more successful and expensive, developers have turned their attention to other downtown neighborhoods (see Developers' Perspective, below).

A new park at Surveyors' Point has been designed and HWDDC has a 30-year renewable lease on the land with the county. Funding for park improvements, however, is yet to be obtained. Essentially a leftover triangle of land next to the bridge approach ramp, the site has historic significance as the location of the first surveyor's marker for the city. Located near the north edge of the district, the park will be closest to the National Terminals project (see p. 99). It will provide a needed open space amenity, but is not large enough to offer recreational opportunities.

The most significant unfinished portion of the district consists of the large number of parking lots. These will, of course, require new construction. One quite large lot lies at the district's heart. Another even larger one lies on the edge of the District, tying it to Public Square. In fact, the district's boundaries were drawn to exclude it, since it was at one time destined to support a very large office project that failed when its intended tenant declared bankruptcy. Its development, however, will be crucial to the district since it faces two major streets and

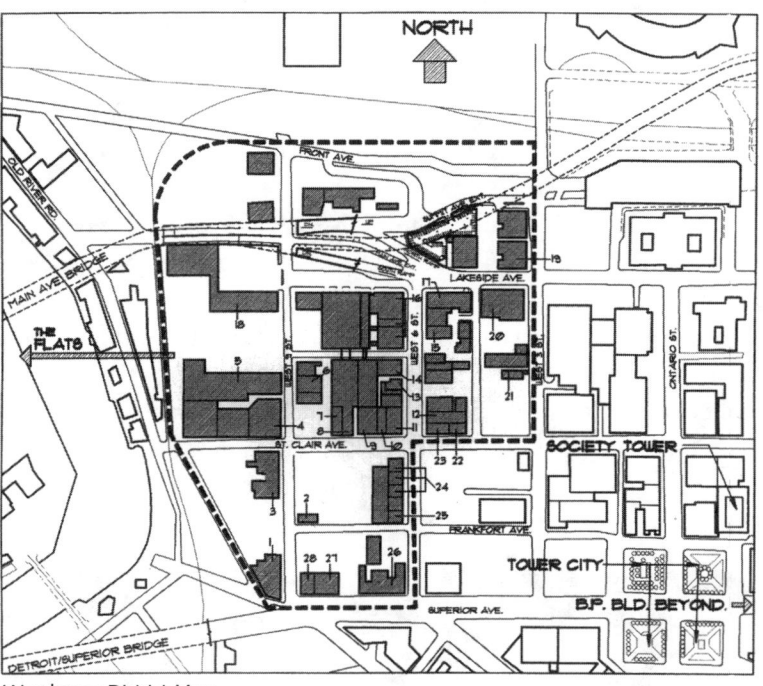

Warehouse District Map

1. Western Reserve Building
2. Hilliard Block
3. Crittenden Block/Crittenden Ct. Apts.
3a. Lorenzo Carter Building
4. Otis Terminal/*William Edwards Building*
5. Bingham Building
6. Bloch Block and Miller Building
7. George Worthington Building
8. Gilcrest Building
9. Joseph and Feiss Building
10. Hoyt Atrium/Garretson's Building
11. Hoyt Block
12. Ace Shoe Building/*Klein-Marks Building*
13. Harry Weinraub
14. New York Coach Building/*Mill Distributors*
15. Hat Factory
16. Root-McBride/Bradley Buildings
17. 425 Lakeside/*Stone Block*
18. National Terminals
19. Courthouse Square/*Crown Building*
20. Lakeside Place/*L.N. Gross Company*
21. Wohl's/*Lawyer's Building*
22. Grand Arcade/City Mission
23. Waring Block
24. Johnson Block
25. L.F. & S. Burgess Grocers Building
26. Rockefeller Building
27. Perry-Payne Building
28. 820 Building/*Brotherhood of Railroad Trainmen*
29. Water Street Apartments/*Bardons & Oliver Building*

will give shape to the transition between the district and downtown. While the HWDDC does not have jurisdiction over the property, the City appears to be sensitive to the necessity of coordinating development review with HWDDC. The owner of one of the other large parcels within the district is said to be considering a project that would include a residential tower surrounded by townhouses appropriate to the historic district in scale and design. Retail would not be included, since demand for that type of space is limited.

Among HWDDC's current initiatives are the formation of a Special Improvement District (SID) and the creation of a program for historic conservation easements. The SID is very similar to the business improvement districts in other parts of the country, but has only recently been authorized by law in Ohio and HWDDC will be one of the first SIDs in Cleveland. The SID will be a self-taxing district providing a stable revenue stream for HWDDC to use for security services, street cleaning, and other improvements. While the local property owners expressed mixed reactions to the SID, it was generally viewed as a positive step toward stabilizing the improvement of the area.

Historic conservation easements are a new tool in the Cleveland area, and are intended to encourage owners of historic structures to donate an easement in perpetuity to HWDDC for the conservation of historically significant portions of their buildings. This will allow them to qualify for additional special tax benefits. This innovative program will have the dual benefits of protecting historic features such as facades and interiors and making it more financially feasible to renovate historic buildings.

Quality of Buildings, Renovations and Urban Design

The district's historic building stock consists, with considerable variation, of generally high quality structures. Renovations have achieved varying levels of quality depending on the owner and architect — some are excellent and some are rather mediocre. Overall, however, the impact of the renovations is quite positive. All were subject to design review by the HWDDC, Cleveland's

A block of Warehouse District buildings before restoration

A block of Warehouse District buildings after renovation

Landmarks Commission, the Ohio State Historic Preservation Office and the National Park Service.

The most serious detraction to the physical environment is the series of large open parking lots, created by the earlier demolition in the area, at the district's center and downtown edge. Although master planning and urban design guidelines for the City envision future mixed use development on those sites, currently they are a significant gap in the district's urban fabric.

In addition, other than street trees, which have been planted at regular intervals throughout the district, the street improvements are very spotty, done only in a few areas (primarily West Sixth Street). Where paving has been done, it covers only part of the sidewalks, and the sandstone is not holding up well (it is cracking and exfoliating). Historically styled lights have been installed in only a few locations, though Cleveland Public Power Company is now providing them throughout the district. Signage was inconsistent, though there are signs with a logo and text identifying the Warehouse District. Street signs have received no special treatment. All new signs go through design review and Cleveland Landmarks approval. Each project is reviewed individually. A downtown master signage program for street signs, locators, and kiosks has been approved by the City for implementation in 1998.

Bradley Building after renovation

Case Study: Bradley Building, West Sixth and Lakeside
Actually three buildings, the complex includes the Bradley Building, built in 1887 and the Root-McBride and Cobb's Buildings built in 1884. The project was the district's first adaptive reuse/mixed use project, finished in 1984 by a developer who still lives in the building. At the time the district was still mostly abandoned, so this was clearly a pioneer project. It consists of 38 large apartments (able to be bigger than those created today because of what were then lower costs), office space, and ground floor retail in 152,000 square feet on eight floors. While the building's first tenants were artists and "vanguards," it now has tenants more typical of the district.

Case Study: Worthington Square and the
URS Building, St. Clair Avenue at West Sixth
Completed in 1996, this mixed use project combines two buildings from 1873 and 1878. It consists of 40,000 square feet, with five floors of offices, plus 52 apartments and ground floor retail. The project attracted a large architectural/engineering firm (URS Consultants) from the suburbs. It cost about $12.5 million and included financing from Cleveland Tomorrow, a UDAG grant and bond financing from the City.

Case Study: Perry-Payne, Superior Avenue near West Ninth
Built in 1887 as a prestigious office building, and designed by leading Cleveland architects (Cudell and Richardson), this is one of the finer and more highly decorated structures in the district. Renovated in 1996 at a cost of approximately $9 million, it consists of 100,000 square feet on eight floors which have been converted into 93 residential lofts and 8,000

Perry-Payne building

square feet of ground floor retail, currently accommodating an upscale billiards hall.

Case Study: Crittenden Court Apartments, West Ninth near St. Clair

This project is located at the western edge of the district on a slope that leads down toward the flats, close to the light rail stop. An archeological dig conducted on the site in 1994 found the foundations of two houses from the 1830s as well as remains from pharmaceutical industry activities. The project itself, completed in 1996, was the first apartment building constructed in downtown in over 30 years. It consists of 208 units with ground floor retail and an attached parking structure. It was represented as having demonstrated the demand for housing at this density in the downtown area; however, for several people we interviewed, its design review process left something to be desired. Although the review led to some improvements (including changing from a sloped to a flat roof more like the warehouses and the re-proportioning of windows to make them more sympathetic to surrounding buildings), the project was under great pressure to gain approvals in order to qualify for federal funds that would otherwise have been lost. In the event, the project was sited, configured and detailed in a ways that could have been greatly improved. However, locals seemed to agree that, given the circumstances and pressures to allow it move forward, it was the best that could have been achieved.

Crittendon Court Apartments rendering

Case Study: National Warehouse Terminals Apartments, West Ninth to West Tenth at Lakeside

This significant project was nearing completion at the time of the site visit. The 500,000 square foot terminal building dates from the early 1900s and was the largest refrigerated warehouse in the region. It consists of 248 units plus upper ground floor retail on West Tenth Street and a number of amenities. Its recreated water tower serves as the project's logo. It is being renovated by the Alexander Company of Madison, Wisconsin which was brought in after local attempts to finance and complete the project had failed (the prior owner was in federal tax court). One special aspect of the project is its use of federal low income tax credit financing requiring a percentage of low and moderate income "affordable" units (at 60% of county income levels — which are higher than city incomes). 110 units of affordable housing will be mixed indistinguishably with market rate units. Cost of the project is about $27 million, or about $70,000 per unit. Among the eleven layers of financing are an equity contribution of $8.5 million from corporate partner Kimberly-Clark, revenue bonds, and loans from the City and from Cleveland Tomorrow, as well as $4.4 million in historic tax credits.

National Warehouse Terminals

Case Study: Kirkham Place Townhomes, West 10th Street

Six units of new housing for sale are being built by HWDDC, essentially as a demonstration

Kirkham Place townhouses rendering

that demand exists for this type of accommodation. These will be the first fee-simple residential units built in downtown in over 100 years. On an infill lot, these townhouses will have about 2,500 square feet and sell for about $275,000. All six are already reserved without marketing or publicity. While we were not able to study the project's design in detail, it appears to have taken a limited number of elements from the historic structures, but interpreted them in a current design vocabulary.

Moving the City Mission

One of the institutions located in the district before its redevelopment was a homeless mission, which found the area to be an appropriate location for serving its clientele. When a developer offered to purchase its building with the intent of renovation, the City Mission Inc. did a feasibility study which showed that it would be better served to take the money raised through the sale (together with added fundraising) and invest in creating a new campus on another edge of downtown. We were told that city agencies assisted in the negotiations with that community to help gain acceptance for the plan. Questions about the possibility that the mission was forced out in the face of gentrification were answered clearly and consistently – it was not the case. In fact, there was no community of residents in the district that could have been displaced by its redevelopment – almost no one lived there. The community which now inhabits the district has been newly created by the actions supported by HWDDC.

Who Lives in the District

Housing in the district is competing effectively with Cleveland's close-in suburban apartments. In fact, demand is so strong that the Warehouse District has one of the lowest vacancy rates in the city (under four percent at the time of our visit) and commands higher rents than comparable housing in the suburbs.

The first wave of residents are mainly young single people and older couples ("empty nesters") who are attracted to the district for its convenience and amenities. The target tenant to date has been a moderate-to-middle income person who may work in or near downtown. Developers and building managers report the surprising statistic that approximately 50% of their tenants are new or returning to Cleveland (many from out of state) and that 25% of the tenants do not work in the downtown but reverse commute. The first low-to-moderate income housing is about to be completed, which will broaden the income range of residents.

The more recent thrust within the Warehouse District is to develop for-sale housing to attract longer-term, more stable residents and families to the area (see case study on Kirkham Place). Family oriented amenities, such as recreational open space and schools, do not yet exist in the district so presumably most of this housing will be for childless households. This kind of housing is consistent with the Mayor's objective of bringing higher income people back into the city in order to create a residential community with economic diversity in the downtown. However, it is an untested market, and the small size of the project does not adequately establish the depth of demand. Nonetheless, more such housing is in the concept stage of development.

The Historic Warehouse District as a Neighborhood

The Warehouse District can be characterized as an emerging neighborhood, already offering significant amenities to those who live there, but likely to improve as new projects are completed and more people are there to support added services. Prior to renovations, there was almost no one living in the area; today approximately 1,000 people live in the district and this number will grow to 1,500 when current projects come on line in the next year or two. The Warehouse District and the City of Cleveland are actively encouraging the mix of uses which will support long-term residential use in the downtown and create a "24 hour" city.

The position of the Warehouse District offers unique amenities to residents. It is located at the historic center of downtown Cleveland, with views toward Lake Erie, the Cuyahoga River, and Public Square. Downtown offices, Society Tower and the newly renovated train station, Tower City, with its attached upscale retail complex, the courthouse, and major public buildings are all within walking distance. The "Flats" (formerly industrial flat land at the base of the hill) is increasingly the site of restaurants and nightclubs which are infiltrating under-used industrial buildings. The Natural Science Museum and Rock and Roll Hall of Fame, as well as major sports complexes, are also close by.

All these features offer a high quality of life for new downtown residents and a destination for the city and the region. We were told that the downtown was completely lacking in evening activities prior to redevelopment of the Warehouse District and the flats.

High-end retail shopping is directly adjacent at Public Square but at the current time there is only one small grocery store in the district; larger scale grocery shopping must be done by car or transit. Other residential services such as laundries or drug stores are lacking and will require more residents to support them. There is a small park adjacent to the new transit station just below the district, and Public Square near the downtown, but there is currently no major green space within the district itself (see What is Planned, above). Thus, amenities that could attract families, such as outdoor recreation or schools, do not yet exist in the district.

Role of the City vis-a-vis Other Players

Cleveland is, in many ways, recovering well from its relatively recent financial and leadership crisis of the mid-1970s. In fact, the early move for preservation of the district coincided with the beginning of civic recovery in the late 1970s and early 1980s and provided the supports necessary for redevelopment to occur.

Following the period of demolition in the 1970s, master planning for the Warehouse District was initiated by HWDDC. The Master Plan they developed in the mid-1980s was adopted in 1991 into the city master plan entitled Vision 2000, which itself was developed by the Cleveland Planning Commission and by Cleveland Tomorrow, an independent economic development organization representing the interests of the city's largest corporations. The City's planning effort was spearheaded by private organizations, due in part to the fact that the City was in financial disarray and could not have undertaken a planning effort at that time. Beginning with the election of Mayor Voinovich (now governor) and current Mayor Michael R. White, planning and economic development have again become priorities.

In recent years, the Planning and Community Development Departments have worked closely with HWDDC and with others involved in promoting the redevelopment of the Warehouse District. The City has made downtown housing a priority and the Community Development Department has created a Downtown Housing office which assists the district in facilitating the financing, development, and marketing of housing in the area. The City's philosophy is to support developers and development groups whose projects are consistent with these planning objectives. In the case of the Community Development Department, the City has a more direct role through lending and financing initiatives under its control. The Director of Planning estimates that the City has invested upward of $30 million in a variety of programs in the area.

While the planning function continues to be carried out by the private sector, it is now with the cooperation of and input from the City. HWDDC is currently updating its 1991 plan, which will in turn be incorporated into the update of the city master plan. That plan, called Civic Vision 2000 and Beyond, is a major planning effort being overseen by the City and Cleveland Tomorrow.

Given the City contributions, including property tax abatements, it is somewhat surprising that no "hard" data are assembled on the economic impacts of this investment in the Warehouse District. The immediate benefits to the city, particularly of housing and retail, are very significant in terms of sales tax revenues and especially income taxes (2% on the personal income of residents — a tremendous incentive for the City to attract new residents). However, the perception of all involved seems to be that property values of the neighborhood are increasing and, thus, that the city will benefit eventually. Increased property values, along with the other revenues and benefits, appears to more than justify City investments in the district.

Financing

Each of the projects in the district has had to create its own financial package involving multiple lenders and sources of funds. One developer described this as "layer cake" financing, another as "baklava" financing. Early support came from local labor union pension funds, as unions saw the projects' potential to create jobs for their members. At first it was necessary to find mostly non-commercial sources of financing. Now that the area has an established track record, banks will lend a higher percentage of the total package.

However, a few banks were willing to take some risk rather early on (mid-1980s) for several reasons: they perceived that something needed to happen in the area, some projects seemed to make financial sense, and the developer who approached them initially was well known to them and willing to sign a personal guarantee (pledging other assets if these projects failed). The personal guarantee suggests that the banks were hardly putting themselves at risk; however, once the district was more established and the risks reduced, such pledges became less necessary.

Some of the special financing programs that have been used in the area include the following (from the HWDDC draft Master Plan of 1997):

Property tax abatement This device requires a "but for" justification — but for the abatement the project would not be viable). These offer up to 100% abatement on improvements: historic improvements can be abated for up to 20 years and residential improvements for 10 to 15 years, depending on their scale.

Historic rehabilitation tax credit This is a 20% income tax credit if the project qualifies by National Park Service standards through being individually listed on the National Register of Historic Places or contributing to the district (which is listed).

UDAG (HUD Urban Development Action Grant) Redirect. These funds were left over from a project that did not proceed and have been used as City loans which can be recycled to other projects after they are paid off.

Street corner within the Warehouse District

HUD Section 108 loan guarantees These come through the City Department of Economic Development for residential projects.

Low Income Tax Credits These are currently being used on the first such project in the district (National Terminals — see case study, above).

Outright low interest loans This type of loan comes from the City and from Cleveland Tomorrow.

(NB: In the last year the City Council has lowered the tax abatement available to projects, and has asked for annual review of net revenues to assess whether the abatement level should be lowered.)

The Developers' Perspective

Five of the area's developers, including pioneers and a recent arrival from out of town, told us how helpful HWDDC has been in expediting their projects and in supporting the evolution of the district. They described a highly effective spirit of cooperation in Cleveland, where the relevant city agencies work together to expedite projects that contribute to the city's overall objectives. This was said to be very different from other cities as well as from the atmosphere in Cleveland before about 1980.

The developers also described the risks and potential rewards of working in the Warehouse District. In terms of risks, some are inherent to rehabilitation projects where one simply does not know all the problems that will have to be solved until work starts. More significantly for the pioneers, there was no established market in this area. They had to believe in a vision and take risks which made it especially difficult to obtain financial backing early on. More recently, however, they feel that the vision has become reality in that the district is now an attractive market, in some ways stronger than the rental market in the suburbs. Higher rents allow them either to make profits on older projects or to justify higher costs for current projects. The developers were clear that rehabilitated historic properties offer highly attractive features that new construction cannot achieve. These include more space and higher ceilings as well as special historical details.

All of the projects have had to cobble together financing from many sources (see section on financing), resulting in complicated deals which require considerable effort to put together. Given the limited number of properties which are appropriate for rehabilitation in the district, several of the developers see opportunity shifting to other parts of downtown where there are buildings that are easier to rehabilitate.

The Foundations' Perspective

This project benefited greatly from well timed but modest infusions of support from several local foundations. We interviewed representatives of three foundations which were centrally involved in the evolution of the district: the Chilcote, Cleveland, and Murphy foundations. These foundations appear to perceive the redevelopment of the district as important to the whole city and see HWDDC as a most capable agent for achievement of this goal. The foundations have played an important role in supporting HWDDC's general operations and many of its initiatives, though they do not fund the actual redevelopment work. The foundations also appear to be committed to continued support for appropriate initiatives.

Assessing Project Success

How Well It Met Its Own Goals

- *To stop the demolition of historic buildings and develop mechanisms to protect and rehabilitate them.*
  HWDDC, together with the city, has been effective at stopping demolition of historic buildings and it is reasonable to presume that, barring exceptional circumstances, no more will be lost. This has dramatically reversed the situation that existed before

1980 when almost half the historic buildings were lost, many of them becoming parking lots.

HWDDC has been very active in developing mechanisms to protect and rehabilitate remaining buildings. These include the survey and master plan it prepared, participation in getting the district and individual buildings listed on the National Register of Historic Places, development and implementation of design guidelines and reviews, facilitating other agency reviews, and assisting with finding financing. In addition, they are developing an innovative historic conservation easement which will contribute to the preservation of historic features and make it easier for owners to rehabilitate and maintain their buildings.

- *To clean up blight caused by a concentration of under-utilized warehouse buildings*
  While in a few areas there are still a fair number of buildings which have not been rehabilitated, it would no longer be accurate to describe the district itself as blighted. It appears that HWDDC has succeeded in cleaning up the blight. On the other hand, some of the remaining buildings will probably take many years to find appropriate uses and sources of funding for their rehabilitation, so there will be "holes" in the district's urban fabric for some time.

- *To create a mixed use residential neighborhood in the heart of downtown*
  The project has already succeeded to a significant degree in creating a real downtown neighborhood; when current projects bring almost 50% more residents in the next two years it will become even more vibrant. Residential amenities, however, are limited to a single convenience store.

  Mixed with mostly professional offices, there are many restaurants, bars and clubs, as well as some destination retail establishments (including galleries) which draw downtown workers and suburbanites – a situation that is reported to be completely changed from 10 years ago when there was nothing happening downtown after 5 pm. Now, on weekend nights, there are people coming in and out of restaurants and bars, enlivening the street scene. There are, however, only a limited number of neighborhood commercial services.

- *To attract middle class people back to the city*
  The Historic Warehouse District has attracted a significant number of middle class people back to the city. Most are young professionals and empty nesters who appreciate the lifestyle. Half are new or returning Cleveland residents who want an urban experience and many reverse commute or work downtown without needing a car. The resident profile will become more diverse in the future — at both ends of the spectrum — with the first use of low income tax credits in the district and the new emphasis on building housing for sale. Since no low income (or other) people lived in the district prior to redevelopment, gentrification was not an issue.

How Well It Met Selection Committee Concerns

- *Is enough done yet; has it achieved critical mass?*
  While still very much in transition, and with much yet to be accomplished, the Historic Warehouse District is coming together as a place and as a neighborhood. It is already an attractive area to live, to work, and to visit – and will improve with projects that are underway or soon to start. All this is to the great credit of HWDDC, the City, and the other participants.

  On the other hand, there are reasons to believe that some large buildings that have not been rehabilitated will take a long time to be completed, as they pose more challenges than properties in other parts of downtown. Also crucial to the evolution of the district will be the disposition of parking lots within and bordering it. One very large lot provides the transition between the district and downtown and the way it is handled will have a very major impact on the district, visually and as a place to live. There are currently no concrete plans for its development.

- *Has the district had an impact on the surrounding area or on the balance of downtown?*
The district is credited with demonstrating that there is demand for downtown housing and for amenities such as restaurants and specialty shops that can attract visitors from the metropolitan area and the region. In this way, the district has helped to generate renewal in other in-town neighborhoods (e.g., Gateway), and is also providing organizational and programmatic models (such as the special improvement district and the historic conservation easement) which others are expected to emulate.

- *What is the design quality of the original structures and the renovations?*
The quality of the structures and the renovations vary considerably. Some original buildings are of exceptional architectural quality, while others are plain. Similarly, the design quality of historic renovation is uneven. The review process and the assistance offered with preservation and adaptive reuse have been helpful in improving the quality of what was done.

- *Are services provided? Are they adequate?*
City services are generally adequate, though the district is planning to improve on some of them — especially security and street cleaning — through the implementation of a Special Improvement District.

Watercolor of the Warehouse District, by local artist Marylou Ferbert

Values, Appropriateness and Quality of the Process and Place

After recovering from its fiscal and leadership crisis of the 1970s, the City of Cleveland appears to have become an excellent model of cooperation among agencies, public and private, and varied interests. They have structured a coordinated approach to redevelopment, downtown housing, and economic development which may be a model for other areas. Foundations, private not-for-profit organizations, and private developers appear to work together well toward common goals. We found no evidence of elitism, gentrification, or displacement.

Leadership Effectiveness

HWDDC is led by an active board of trustees who contribute greatly to its success. Staff is well qualified, knowledgeable, effective and respected by all the relevant players. The organization appears to have been very successful at handling leadership succession, both on the board and among staff.

Prospects for Sustainability

While the district has achieved critical mass, has many positive projects underway, and seems to have the needed support of governmental and private entities who recognize its importance, there are still some ways in which it may be vulnerable. The two main issues, already mentioned above, are the somewhat problematic remaining historic structures and the large scale surface parking lots. These will have to get effective attention over the next five to ten years in order for the quality and vitality of the district to be improved and even sustained.

Selection Committee Comments

The Selection Committee applauded the many achievements of the HWDDC, but viewed the district as a work in progress whose long term success will depend on the resolution of some critical issues — especially the disposition of the large unfinished areas within it. Only then will it be possible to understand how the district will function and to assess its lasting impact on the city of Cleveland. While it was clear to the Committee that the district is playing a role in Cleveland's comeback, they wondered how important it was compared to other projects like the Rock and Roll Hall of Fame or Jacobs field.

The City of Cleveland was recognized by the Committee as having made important contributions to the Warehouse District in recent years. However, the Committee felt that, in its period of decline, the City had shared responsibility for the deterioration of the fabric of the neighborhood (having taken actions that encouraged and allowed indiscriminate demolition) and that its support for turning the district around was not as strong as it might have been in terms of leadership, financial incentives, and direct investment (e.g., in street improvements or parks).

Aerial view of the District, showing surface parking lots.

The Committee compared the Warehouse District to others they were familiar with, such as Lowertown in Saint Paul and concluded that, while the district was generally well done, it had not yet realized its potential in terms of coherent vision, urban impact, or quality of design. In particular, while some of the individual projects within the district were recognized as being of high quality, in others the Committee noted a certain lack of consistency in design.

Despite these concerns, the Committee was impressed with the ongoing contributions and innovations of the HWDDC and its present cooperative relationship with the City, which made the Committee feel that there was a good likelihood that the district would meet its future challenges.

Reference

Christopher Johnston, "The Revitalizing Warehouse District," *Urban Land*, April 1996, pp. 46–47.

For More Information

Historic Warehouse District Development Corporation
614 Superior Avenue, N.W.
Suite 714
Cleveland, OH 44113

TEL: 216-344-3937
FAX: 216-344-3962

WEBSITE: www.warehousedistrict.org

**What Was Learned
About Urban Excellence**

RUDY
BRUNER
AWARD

FOR URBAN
EXCELLENCE

Vision

To make an excellent urban place requires a vision, a dream, the invention of a new concept or the combination of elements in a way never previously tried. It is an arena in which creativity and imagination are critical, and a lifetime of preparation may converge with circumstances that allow a new concept to take root.

Some commentators suggest that urban change is the product of large social, economic and historical forces, more than the actions of individuals. Certainly this process describes common trends that are taking place in cities around the country or around the world (such as densification of the center, or growth around the periphery). Others focus on change as the product of individual creative actions, great leaps — even genius — that give shape to the larger forces. The extraordinary individuals can create concepts or forms that may become models that are emulated elsewhere. Among the 1997 Rudy Bruner Award winners, creative individuals worked within the context of what was possible – and then moved beyond that context to create new, and even myth-shattering models of urban excellence.

As the Selection Committee reflected on and discussed the criteria they might apply in choosing this round's winners, creativity and entrepreneurial vision were among the most important issues raised. In effectively applying this entrepreneurial spirit in the public or not-for-profit sectors, the creativity, strength of commitment, and drive to see the goal accomplished mirrored that often seen in the private sector. This entrepreneurial vision provides a guiding concept for the complex and difficult process of bringing a project to reality. While an enormous amount of effort and resources may have to be marshaled to implement a new vision, it is the creative vision that guides the process and gives it its unique and powerful identity.

Project Row Houses opens up its doors.

One Selection Committee member stated that "change in cities is often attributable to a couple of people who do something, and everything spins around it. And…often it's something you figure can't actually be done, but they do it anyway." Another added, "It's something that is just truly unlikely [but], because it's…a passionate vision of some individual, they manage to change the way things were getting done for the better."

A Selection Committee member described the kinds of significant outcomes such innovative projects can have: "It could have changed the psychology of the town, it could have changed people's attitudes towards investment in an area, it could have changed their behavioral patterns about using part of the city. It could have been a model for other cities, and…have an impact beyond [its own locale]."

To become such a model, it may be necessary to move beyond existing, dominant concepts or even myths about what is possible. (Can assisted housing succeed at the scale of 600 rooms? Can art form the basis for community transformation? Can an arts complex rejuvenate downtown?). The leaders of these winning projects believed passionately in the transformative power of their values and ideas and they were prepared either to convince others that new models could succeed or to proceed with or without traditional means of support.

A meaningful, creative, or new vision for a city addresses a real need, but approaches it in a new way and, in so doing, extends the notion of what is possible. If it works, it can become a new model for others to emulate. The Selection Committee looked for projects that only happened because of the energy, creativity and vision brought by an individual or group, and that demonstrated a strong positive outcome or result.

This entrepreneurial, creative spirit is necessary in order to take risks and try new and unproven approaches to the often intractable problems of big cities. While city bureaucracies are not necessarily the locus where one would expect to find this spirit, for several of the projects the city officials did contribute sufficiently to supporting the vision (New York City, Oakland). In others there was less support, and the city may at times even have been an obstacle for the project to overcome (Houston).

The Selection Committee discussed at some length the question of how a creative vision comes to shape the city – should it come from a strong leader or should it be based on participation and consensus? Here, the Committee was interested in the balance between "top-down" and "bottom-up" processes. While it recognized the contributions and even charisma of some of the project leaders, it also noted the importance of democratic and participatory processes. One Committee member commented that "there has got to be a balance —and I think we are seeing this with some of the visionary entrepreneurs in these projects — between vision and…consensus-building with the public." Another recognized the need to work "bottom-up and top-down simultaneously."

The Committee was also interested in the organizational (and often political) skills needed to mobilize others toward realization of the vision. The projects that proceeded most expeditiously and with the fewest obstacles were those where strong links were developed and maintained by the leader(s) to others in their organizations and to community and civic agencies. Realizing the vision and keeping it alive through the inevitable struggles requires determination, gumption, drive, and follow through — as well as the support of others and of the broader political milieu.

Three of the projects were envisioned by individuals or small groups who created powerful new concepts of what could be done in their cities, while the other two are touched by vision and entrepreneurial energy in more modest ways.

The Times Square is the product of one woman's powerful vision of turning a nearly derelict structure with a history of failed proposals into the largest supportive housing facility in the country. This required Rosanne Haggerty to challenge myths about the limits to the scale on which this type of serviced housing facility could be successfully operated and the types of population that could be successfully mixed. She had to convince sitting tenants, powerful neighbors, a panoply of city boards, financial institutions and labor unions to back the project (or at least not to block it). It is even more impressive that all this was done in New York City, with its massive needs and equally imposing obstacles to accomplishment.

Project Row Houses is the product of Rick Lowe's unique vision of art transforming not only a set of historic "shotgun" houses but a neighborhood as well. Before discovering the row

Rosanne Haggerty, The Times Square

Tony Hannigan, Center for Urban Community Services

houses, Lowe was already committed to finding ways to reconnect the African-American community to art and to its cultural roots. Lowe believes that art in a community setting has the potential to transform that community by creating positive cultural images of ethnic identity – through showcasing the accomplishments of African-American artists, by getting community people involved in artistic expression, and by engaging people from within and without the community in a dialogue about issues raised by the art itself. This radically different approach had to be accomplished outside of traditional funding streams, through foundations and volunteers. As the project became a reality, it evolved in response to circumstances and opportunities, growing to incorporate housing for young, single mothers and daycare as well as a wide variety of arts projects.

The Center in the Square. It is clearly a novel gesture to use an arts complex as the impetus for renewal of a declining downtown. This notion appears to have been born partly from the confluence of propitious circumstances (a theater needing a new home,

Rick Lowe, Founder, Project Row Houses

considerable attention focused on the market area near downtown, and a city-wide participatory planning event) and partly from the vision of a small group of civic leaders to locate several arts organizations in the area. In addition, there were pioneering businesses and real estate investors who took considerable risks in being among the first to move into the area, when the Center was no more than a plan on paper.

Hismen Hin-Nu realizes a vision of a dense, mixed-use project on what had been an underutilized retail site. The plan began with a study of the neighborhood by a group of architecture and planning students. It was adopted by the city and the not-for-profit developer, EBALDC. Then it was given shape through an open, participatory design process involving all the parties and led by the project architect. The authorship of the project is broadly shared, and the execution was skillful. EBALDC itself is an entrepreneurial organization, seeing needs and opportunities in the economic development area and moving strongly to expand training and opportunities for its tenants and other clients.

Cleveland Historic Warehouse District found its origins in a classical battle to preserve an important historical building which was threatened with imminent demolition. Winning that battle emboldened the group to broaden its vision and try to save what was left of the entire district. Again, a few urban pioneers moved into the district in its very early days and individual entrepreneurs forged ahead to renovate properties well before the banks or other traditional financing sources would support them.

Art In the City

This year's winners revealed a great deal about the transformative power of art in the urban environment. Art is central to three of the five projects (**Project Row Houses, Center in the Square,** and **Hismen Hin-Nu**) — and important to the other two (**The Times Square** and the **Historic Warehouse District**).

The predominance of art in these projects gave the Selection Committee the opportunity to discuss the role of art in urban excellence. The Committee found that art can be a strong force for revitalization. It can be an integrative factor, bringing diverse people together; it can be transformative of a project or an area or for the people involved in it; and it can provide images that express multiple levels of meaning about urban life, culture and places.

Because of the way a project makes high quality art accessible, people may be attracted to a part of the city (downtown or a neighborhood) they would never otherwise have visited. They may meet and interact with people they otherwise wouldn't have — artists or members of other ethnic or socio-economic groups. This is the case for Project Row Houses and Center in the Square.

People may become involved with art as an activity, or observe or interact with artists in a way that increases understanding or adds meaning (or self-esteem) to their lives. In some instances, art and artists who create it can provide important models of cultural identity. Over time and on a large enough scale, the involvement can become meaningful to the community, galvanizing energy and breaking barriers. This is true at Project Row Houses, Center in the Square, and The Times Square.

Art may be incorporated into a building or urban area in a way that the occupants and neighbors can enjoy and admire it and, if it is powerful and relevant, it can add meaning or understanding of the project to those who use it. We found this at Project Row Houses, Hismen Hin-Nu and, to some extent, at The Times Square.

For **Project Row Houses** art, and especially that of African-American artists, is the unifying theme of the place. The project has the lofty aspiration of using the experience and production of art to raise important questions and to effect people's lives. It also uses artists' (and other volunteers') energy to transform a group of decaying houses of historical value into a vibrant center for its community. Art is put to work on many levels — it is on display and being created; African-American artists are present in the community while their work is being displayed, providing important role models for community residents; and the row houses themselves can be considered as art and have been used as the subject of paintings.

Rick Lowe and others there believe that art can change lives, bringing hope, meaning, and a renewal of the spirit. It is seen as catalytic and transformative, having special power in a disenfranchised community to tap and inspire the creativity that is lurking unexpressed or undiscovered. Art can even be a tool for "community building," increasing individual self-esteem and a sense of pride in the community and its cultural heritage. The project also encourages pride in the community's heritage, making the houses stand as symbols of its root values, struggles, and accomplishments. The Selection Committee was impressed that unlike many community or public art projects that are single episodes of short duration, "It's a permanent public art project in the community.

Floyd Newsum's "Tribal Markings" at Project Row House

They're always there." Another Selection Committee member commented that, "All of a sudden you've got large numbers of people marching into the Third Ward.... [and] the stereotypical view of that part of the world is changing."

At **Center in the Square**, the location and synergy of five cultural and arts organizations are used to draw people to downtown and have had the effect of transforming a decaying market area into an intensely used attraction. The institutions include an art museum, a theater and the regional arts association. The Center brought the art museum to downtown from an elite, rather remote, and ethnically homogeneous neighborhood. Its displays are now more diverse and culturally relevant, including ethnic art (such as a collection of African masks), and its attendance has broadened and increased many-fold. The institutions also offer hands-on art classes for children, as well as outreach programs for the region's schools. As a result of the Center, the level of cultural opportunities is very high for a city the size of Roanoke and the reach is very broad. The draw of these institutions has also contributed greatly to the transformation of the market area – from a run down and partially abandoned corner of the downtown into a vibrant, pedestrian-oriented zone with a critical mass of shops, restaurants and entertainment.

Hismen Hin-Nu was able to incorporate meaningful public art at a scale and to an effect well beyond what is usually possible in a lower income housing project. In fact, a hallmark of the project is the incorporation of art into the design. A $50,000 National Endowment for the Arts grant was obtained with the intent of using the art not only as decoration, but to symbolize the racial and cultural diversity, and unity of the area. Artists representing various racial groups were invited to make submissions. The architect said: "The coexistence of art from these diverse traditions inspires a spirit of cooperation not only among the tenants but in the community." Examples include frieze panels at the tops of the

A painted mural on Hismen Hin-nu speaks to the multi-cultural character of the neighborhood and can be seen from the BART trains passing by.

towers which weave together patterns from many cultures, and a band of tiles along the street which represent 22 distinct cultures. Most notable is the sunburst gate and entry arch which provide an image that is appropriate to and inclusive of the entire community. The design is a highly imageable creation which inspired the name of the project.

The **Cleveland Historic Warehouse District** worked with the citywide Committee for Public Art to add art to the streets of the new downtown neighborhood. Examples include a national competition for the West Sixth Streetscape which resulted in sculptures inspired by the district's history of warehousing — sculpture consisting of stacks of sandstone blocks usable as seating (which refer to historical images of crates stacked on the sidewalks); "Art Behind Bars" which entailed installations behind the security bars in street level windows of an old warehouse; and "Signs of Life" which fostered collaborations between artists and businesses to create inventive and expressive street signs for a number of shops. These projects contributed to the meaning of the district and drew people there to see them.

The Times Square is involved with art on two levels. On the one hand, the meticulous restoration of the beautifully crafted original lobby creates a setting which represents a respect for visual and aesthetic quality. The grand marble staircase, period lighting fixtures, and polished stone floor in the lobby demonstrate a respect for the craftsmanship inherent in the original building.

In addition, The Times Square has made considerable use of participatory art. It provides art workshops for residents' use and displays the results in the lobby. It also features tiles made by the residents which are incorporated into the 15th floor addition.

Reviewing the winning projects from 1997 reawakens our awareness of the importance of art in urban settings — its power to attract people, to excite them, to transform the physical fabric and the pattern of uses, to help people see the city and their lives in fresh ways, to see new possibilities.

Quality of Place

The 1997 winners have much to teach about the physical and architectural aspects of urban excellence. These places are a reminder that residents and citizens care a great deal about the physical qualities of urban places. Good design, quality materials, and physically beautiful environments that house the entire spectrum of human activity are a critical element of excellent urban places. A beautiful and well-designed space enhances and enlivens a creative vision, and can symbolize the project's meaning and importance.

Outstanding design can take many forms, and the 1997 winners present a varied group of places—old and new, large and small, built from both generous and limited budgets. Yet, each created a successful urban place which builds upon the strengths of its context, is open to and enhances its immediate community, supports and strengthens the programs for which it was designed, and contributes to the revitalization of its urban setting. Together these places confirm the essential connection between good design quality and urban excellence.

The Times Square makes a strong statement about the importance and value of providing beautiful and dignified living environments for all segments of the urban population. The quality design of The Times Square reflects the philosophy underlying this project. The handsome living environment, enriched by the patina of time and history, communicates a sense of permanence and stability which mirrors Common Ground's goals of supporting residents and bringing a sense of dignity to their lives. Just as important, the physical transformation of the building has stabilized an important corner in the heart of Times Square, contributing a handsome entrance on the street and three thriving retail outlets on 8th Avenue and 43rd Street.

The Times Square Lobby is an elegant and striking entry for residents and visitors.

Project Row Houses demonstrates that the impact of the physical place can be as powerful on a modest scale as on a grand one. It shows that quality of place does not depend upon size, the expenditure of vast amounts of money, or luxurious materials. While Project Row Houses is the smallest and simplest of the 1997 winners, it has a beautiful and dignified physical presence which underscores the value and importance of the historic "shotgun" houses, and revitalizes two city blocks.

At Project Row Houses it was essential for restoration to

Restoration at Project Row Houses respects the elegant simplicity of the architecture.

respect the historic simplicity of the row houses. Each was repainted in its original white, retaining the corrugated tin roofs (now tinted with a patina of brown rust) and the narrow front and back stoops in their original form. Similarly, the interior courtyard was cleaned up but not paved, thus maintaining its traditional character. The result is a striking visual presence created through the repetition of simple, pleasing forms. As one Selection Committee member commented, "These are lovely, lovely buildings. It's easy to diminish the aesthetic qualities of this place because it is small — but they are beautiful."

The simplicity of these modest buildings contrasts to their powerful symbolism, both culturally and politically. Culturally, they have represented the emancipation and progress of freed slaves, while politically their restoration stands for a reversal of the long neglect of the culture and heritage of the African-American community.

The handsome architecture of **Hismen Hin-nu** demonstrates the connection between design and urban context (particularly its multi-cultural aspects); the value of a participatory design process; and what can be achieved through the use of local architectural vernacular. It also underscores the importance of quality residential environments at all levels of affordability.

The development of Hismen Hin-Nu reflects a strong tradition of participation by residents in planning for their neighborhoods. The design clearly benefited from participatory, architect-led workshops which explored with residents the kinds of options possible on the site. As an antidote to neighborhood concern about a large-scale affordable housing project being introduced into their neighborhood, the architects were able to incorporate elements of residential design usually associated with single family housing. These include interior porches, separate outside entrances, exterior elevations which provide eyes on the street, outside play space for families and children, and a high degree of individualization of units, consistent with varied family configurations.

Finally, HIsmen Hin-Nu is maintained at a very high level, contributing to the feeling of the place as a permanent dwelling rather than transient low cost housing. The use of quality building materials throughout, but especially at street level, has eased maintenance effort and cost.

Center in the Square restored and built onto an historic structure. Physical design, especially the new entry and circulation space — from which all the institutions can be seen — has created a vital synergy among institutions, strengthening and enlivening each. Together with the adjacent market the Center in the Square has created a new urban focal point whose drawing power transcends any one of its separate elements and has succeeded in bringing people of all ages back to the downtown, supporting the educational and cultural life of the area and enlivening small businesses. While design is a less powerful presence here than The Times Square, Hismen Hin-nu, or Project Row Houses, it makes an important point about the synergies which evolve from shared space.

The **Cleveland Historic Warehouse District** demonstrates that the successful creation of a new downtown neighborhood depends upon the interweaving of a complex web of physical, social and economic factors. The physical and architectural quality of the neighborhood goes beyond the restoration of any particular building and depends instead upon achieving a critical mass of historic buildings, quality architectural restorations, consistency of scale and materials, and the quality of the streetscape and public spaces.

The Warehouse District has begun to achieve these goals. It has preserved and restored a significant number of Victorian warehouses. Although quality of restoration varies among individual buildings, the cumulative result of the restorations is the preservation of a handsome group of structures of compatible scale and materials that form an attractive edge to the downtown, and a critical connection to Cleveland's past.

The long term architectural strength of the Warehouse District, however, is dependent upon several factors. It will be important (and challenging), to preserve and re-use the remaining historic buildings, some of which are very large and in poor condition. It will be even more critical to ensure that future development on the large vacant parcels is well designed, and that it re-enforces the scale, materials and historic context inherent in the District, strengthening the still fragile and emerging residential neighborhood.

Preservation as a Strategy for Change

Preservation, restoration, and adaptive reuse of historically or architecturally significant places was a central theme for four of the five 1997 RBA winners. In Houston, Cleveland, New York City, and Roanoke, efforts to save and restore places with historic and cultural significance were an essential element of the projects, and critical to their success. They teach that making excellent places often involves re-creating and breathing new life into what was once of value in our cities. The re-use of these buildings provides an opportunity to take the best of past urban design and adapt it to current needs and economic realities.

A desire to save important historic buildings was a driving force in the inception of the **Cleveland Historic Warehouse District** and **Project Row Houses.** The people who led these projects had a special interest in saving a group of buildings with architectural, historical and cultural relevance. In each case, the program evolved beyond preserving the buildings as museum pieces, to devising unique ways of re-using them to support and enhance the community and larger urban context.

The Times Square and **Center In the Square** are located in areas that had once been central to the commerce and street life of their cities but had since deteriorated. The preservation and reuse of these buildings contributed significantly to the improvement of the whole area. The original motivation for The Times Square was the creation of a social program for a particular needy population. Preserving the building was not the prime motivation, but important synergies developed between the social service and preservation goals. Preservation and restoration of the building provided beautiful and dignified living environments which became a major element of its success. In Roanoke, preserving the farmers' market area, a place with social, historical and cultural importance, was the most important item on the agenda. Rehabilitating the McGuire Building, which houses Center in the Square, was a way to bring cultural and arts organizations together downtown, and provide an important cornerstone for the market facilities. In all four of these cases, successful efforts to preserve and maintain historic structures and spaces resulted in the creation of places that were pleasing, comfortable and successful in supporting contemporary urban needs.

Restored block, Cleveland Historic Warehouse District

In many cities, historic preservation organizations have only come into being as the result of the loss, or threatened destruction, of a treasured local symbol. This was the case with the **Cleveland Historic Warehouse District**, which was born as the result of a local preservation crisis. For years citizens of Cleveland watched the demolition of some of the finest examples of 19th Century buildings in the downtown area, and their replacement by parking lots. The preservation community was finally able to focus its energy when the Hilliard Building, the oldest building in the downtown area, was threatened. Their success in saving the Hilliard Building led directly to the creation of the Historic Warehouse District Development Corporation, which conducted a survey of the surviving buildings and created an historic district listed on the National Register of Historic Places.

The District's judicious use of design review and support of developers in financing and dealing with red-tape has led to the successful conversion of a number of buildings into apartments and retail uses. Their efforts to save this large group of buildings that were similar in age and style, had a cumulative effect that gives the district a distinctive, distinguished look and feel (see Quality of Place). No one doubts that preservation has been a positive and cost-effective process. The only regret is that it didn't begin earlier, before so many important older structures were demolished and the fabric of the community was seriously compromised by a series of surface parking lots in the heart of the district.

The "shotgun" houses that became the site of **Project Row Houses** in Houston's Third Ward are representative of a historic and culturally important residential form. These buildings are small and unprepossessing, but for many in the neighborhood they are symbolic of an era of progress and independence that followed the freeing of slaves after the Civil War. Their scale and the central courtyard reflect a housing form reminiscent of communal life with African roots. Similarly, their neglect and deterioration was symbolic of the social and economic problems of the Third Ward.

Houston is not known for preservation. Development there has most often been characterized by new construction replacing the old. Moreover, the main constituency for the "shotgun" house building type is the local African-American population—a group which is socially, politically, and economically disenfranchised. The likelihood of imminent demolition of these houses was high and they had become symbols of the neglect experienced by this segment of Houston's population. In a city of jarring discontinuities and juxtapositions, constant demolition and new construction, Project Row Houses presents a face of simplicity, unity of appearance, and recollection of important historical events.

The McGuire Building, which was to become the new home of the **Center in the Square**, was not especially distinguished architecturally, but presented an opportunity to bring cultural and arts programs to a central location downtown. The results were successful beyond the expectations of the original planners. The farmers' market has survived, grown, and thrived, the surrounding area has come to life, and the energy has extended across the railroad tracks to the restoration of the Hotel Roanoke and downtown. Thus, historic reuse has been the spark leading to the revival of Roanoke as an important cultural and educational destination.

Preservation and Urban Excellence

This is not the first year that preservation has been an important aspect of urban excellence as recognized in Rudy Bruner Award finalists. Many past winners, from Pike Place in Seattle to South Beach in Miami and Lowertown in St. Paul, have been based on historic preservation. It is reasonable to ask why preservation is important, why it so often is linked to successful examples of urban excellence, and what lessons can be learned for the future of our cities. There are a number of reasons historic preservation can be critical to urban excellence.

Urban Ecology Preservation can be an efficient use of time and resources. By reusing existing sites, scarce materials can be recycled and the energy costs of demolition avoided. Restorations usually cost less than new construction, and carry with them the patina of age that lends continuity to urban life.

Funding Options Restoring a building with historic value can trigger sources of funding including tax incentives that would otherwise not be available to the project. The Times Square benefited greatly from preservation tax credits which provided significant additional funds for construction and restoration. Preservation-based tax incentives contributed to the viability of projects in Cleveland's Historic Warehouse District, projects that, especially early on, might not otherwise have been able to get off the ground.

Quality of the Historic Building Many older buildings have a level of detail and materials that would be difficult or impossible to reproduce economically in a new building (see Quality of the Place). This is especially true for non-profit corporations, which often have minimal budgets that restrict the level of architectural detail.

Quality of Setting The Times Square, as a result of restoration done with preservation funding and incentives, is clearly superior to typical SROs. For the residents, these attractive spaces demonstrate a concern for their welfare and a respect for their humanity.

Many of the historic warehouses in Cleveland also exhibit an elegance of design and attention to detail lacking in much modern construction. Even where interiors have been gutted for rehabilitation, lobbies and facades present Victorian character for their public face, creating a sense of dignity and historic continuity to the visitor.

Symbolic Aspects of Preservation Places symbolize collective cultural memory of people and events, and saving a building can be a powerful statement of the importance and value of cultural history. The emotional bond that exists as part of the psychological sense of place can be broken when buildings are demolished and landscapes torn apart. People can feel a sense of loss and rootlessness when those familiar places are removed, making new construction feel empty and sterile. By preserving buildings and neighborhoods we also preserve images, symbols and memories that can have strong cultural and emotional significance.

The Roanoke farmers' market and the Hotel Roanoke are good examples of the kind of connection that people make to a place. The market provided more than a place for commerce. It was a social and communal space of the best kind and, in an earlier era, the only place where people of all races freely mixed. The Hotel Roanoke was a symbol of quality and a "world-class" hotel for a small southern city. The deterioration of these areas hurt the image local citizens had of their city and generated pessimism for the future of downtown. Their revival has been a hopeful sign for Roanoke as Center in the Square and the adjacent marketplace continue to thrive, a new sense of urban pride is palpable.

Preservation as an Alternative to Urban Planning Some commentators have suggested that preservation has become a grassroots response to some of the excesses of urban planning, serving as a form of urban planning and zoning by default. In some cases it is a reaction to the vacuum created by a lack of thoughtful urban schemes on a broader scale; in others, an alternative to grandiose urban plans that local residents feel are imposed upon them. Preservation has in some cases become a rallying point for

Roof detail, Project Row Houses

neighborhoods trying to maintain their scale and unity in response to highways, public works or private development. The organizations that coalesce around these issues can serve to channel public efforts to change neighborhoods for the better.

Public/Private Collaboration

The era is past in which government was presumed to be the main force planning and implementing urban change. The recent review of the history of the Rudy Bruner Award winners (*Sustaining Urban Excellence; Learning from the Rudy Bruner Award, 1987–1993,* Bruner Foundation, 1998) found that Rudy Bruner Award winners have frequently been the result of collaborations among groups in the public, not-for-profit, and/or for-profit sectors. (See also *Building Coalitions for Urban Excellence,* Bruner Foundation, 1993.) Most often, non-profit groups were the lead organization and prime developer. This makes sense given the realities of our time. Government agencies at all levels are reducing budgets and devolving power upon localities, while businesses naturally focus on efforts that have profit potential. Typically, that leaves non-profit organizations to address pressing urban needs.

This is clearly the case for all five of the 1997 winners, which were collaborative projects where non-profit organizations had the primary responsibility for initiating and overseeing planning and management. The kind and quality of collaboration with private and public sectors, however, varies considerably. While the actions of city agencies were relevant in all these projects, the city government played an active role in the initial stages only in **New York, Oakland,** and **Roanoke.** Also, while most of the projects had some involvement with private, for-profit organizations, private development was usually a small part of the effort, central only to the **Cleveland Historic Warehouse District**. While the non-profit Warehouse District managed the preservation process, as well as overall planning and organizing strategies, the capital, energy, and risks for each individual project came from developers who were seeking profits by creating rental units in rehabilitated buildings. City government was, in much of the early effort, largely irrelevant. In the midst of Cleveland's fiscal crisis, it practically ceded planning authority to the Historic Warehouse District. Now, however, the city is playing a more important role, particularly in institutionalizing the master plans and encouraging developers.

The involvement of all three sectors was balanced best in **The Times Square**, which was one of things that the Selection Committee found appealing. While conceptual development, energy, and leadership was clearly came from Common Ground, the city of New York played a significant role. The purchase, restoration and conversion would not have been possible without the city's significant SRO loan. New York city agencies and offices, which can be an impediment to non-profit development (see case study of the Greenpoint Manufacturing and Design Center in *Building Coalitions for Urban Excellence,* Bruner Foundation, 1996), were facilitative and supportive. This is most clear in the City's efforts to help Common Ground extend and replicate its success in another building and neighborhood. Private corporations also played a role in The Times Square. The companies that rent the street-level retail space along 8th Avenue or 43rd Street, most prominently Starbucks and Ben & Jerry's, provide jobs for residents of The Times Square, and rental revenue which Common Groun uses for job skills training.

Gretchen Dykstra, DIrector of the Times Square Business Improvement District

Center in the Square is a non-profit organization, founded and operated for the support of non-profit cultural institutions. Private enterprise plays a role largely in the maintenance and operation of the farm stands and in the local businesses whose return has had a positive ripple effect on the neighborhood. The city of Roanoke was somewhat involved, providing UDAG funds and encouraging private investment. It has received a very large return in terms of public benefit provided by Center in the Square and resulting development, from a small public investment.

In **Hismen Hin-nu (Sun Gate Terrace)** The City of Oakland had completed planning studies which targeted the San Antonio district for additional housing and commercial development. The City of Oakland was thus willing to play a key role in facilitating the acquisition of the site by EBALDC. The project was the product of a traditional community development model, although the design process and outcome were exemplary. Private enterprise involvement is limited to the street level shops, which have not, to date, experienced significant success.

Project Row Houses, more than any other winner this year, has been on its own in developing funding and support. It is the least supported by local city government. The city of Houston has at times been a neutral bystander and on other occasions and obstacle to be overcome. Despite the fact that Project Row Houses has received funding through the Houston Council for the Arts, the city has not been a source of significant material support. Project Row Houses has had a positive and ongoing relationship with the corporate world in the form of major volunteer efforts by employees of companies such as AMOCO and Chevron, who have performed hands-on restoration work. Although these relationships appear to be based upon a firm and ongoing commitment from these corporations, there is no continuing relationship in Project Row Houses in which the project directly supports or is supported by revenue from private operations.

In this group of excellent projects the energy, innovation and creativity for urban excellence came largely from those working outside of government agencies and structures. Though there is some evidence of increasing commitment by local government, especially in Cleveland, not-for-profit organizations, in particular, play a special role in coordinating the efforts needed to make these efforts succeed. They are able to avoid the bureaucracy and time frames typical of government agencies, and can act where risks outweigh potential profits for private enterprises.

The most successful and sustainable urban projects may be ones where, as in The Times Square, there is a strong collaboration among non-profit, private and public organizations. New York City has been a supportive and helpful partner in The Times Square, which was also able to harness energy and capital from private operations in support of goals that are not, in and of themselves, profit oriented. Its partnership with Ben and Jerry's has been mutually sustaining, and is a good example of a growing trend among non-profits to find ways to support social services with funds from profit-making activities (see also the case study of New Community Corporation in *Sustaining Urban Excellence; Learning from the Rudy Bruner Award for Urban Excellence, 1987–1993*, Bruner Foundation, 1998, and in *Rebuilding Communities: Re-Creating Urban Excellence*, Bruner Foundation, 1993.).

An important role for government agencies may be in helping non-profits achieve stability and viability, as New York City did for The Times Square. Often the biggest problem of non-profit organizations is finding financial support when they are just starting, before a track record has been established. At several times early in its history, Project Row Houses was perilously close to collapse, in part because of the limited level of help it received from the City of Houston. Center in the Square found ways to develop and survive, with limited help from the city of Roanoke, and more significant help from the state. While in these two cases, the cities were able to gain significant rewards for relatively small investment, it may be reasonable to ask how many other projects, that could have had a positive impact but may have been just a little less hardy, collapsed for lack of initial investment and support? In this era, the role of the city government may rest in being wise about ways to identify those projects with potential and need, and provide the support needed to nourish and sustain them.

Adapting New Models of Urban Placemaking

The ability of a project to serve as a model which can be adapted to other urban settings increases its potential for having an impact on national urban practices, and is an important aspect of urban excellence. While each Rudy Bruner Award winner makes a contribution within its particular setting, its impact grows exponentially when it can be successfully adapted to other urban environments. Meaningful adaptation involves application of the guiding ideas and concepts, not replication of the original project. Simply replicating a project with a "cookie cutter" approach would be to ignore unique local contexts and problems. Instead, process, guiding philosophy and concepts should be redefined in the context of each urban setting, drawing upon the unique cultural and social identity of a city or neighborhood. In this group of winners, several have already demonstrated the adaptability of their models to other sites or cities.

In New York City, **The Times Square** model is being used at Common Ground's new project, the Prince George. This project, currently under construction, will again rehabilitate an attractive historic building to serve a mixed population with permanent housing and supportive social services. It need not be the original project leaders who implement the adaptation of innovative models in other cities. The Mayor of Baltimore has recently sent members of his staff to New York to study the Times Square for the purpose of adapting the model to Baltimore.

The **Project Row House** model links culturally-based artistic talent and leadership with discovery and re-use of local architectural forms. These resources are tapped to celebrate ethnic identity and community pride and to provide programs responsive to local community needs. Project Row Houses has formed a separate organization to offer technical assistance to other inner city neighborhoods interested in their approach. In their own words, "Project Row Houses is establishing a national model for reclamation of inner-city neighborhoods with art as a catalyst to stimulate constructive dialogue addressing cultural, educational and social issues." Projects are already underway in Dallas, the Watts area of Los Angeles, East St. Louis, and Birmingham.

Aspects of **Hismen Hin-nu** that can be effectively adapted to other settings include the innovative participatory process, the inclusion of varied unit configurations, and the effective integration of art which grows out of the ethnic mix of the surrounding neighborhood.

Courtyard at Project Row Houses, with permanent art installation.

The **Cleveland Historic Warehouse District** could serve as a model in many other industrialized cities where changes in economic and manufacturing trends have left historic buildings in prime locations under-used and abandoned. The combination of the adaptive reuse of an entire district of buildings and the concept of creating an entirely new residential neighborhood in the downtown, although not unique, is impressive. (See also the case study on Lowertown in *Building Coalitions for Urban Excellence*, The Bruner Foundation, 1996.) In Cleveland the creative uses of layered financing and strict design review created an operating model of financing and development which have demonstrated success and opened up new ways of thinking about district-wide adaptive re-use.

A number of small cities have looked closely at **Center in the Square**, with an eye toward using its model of concentrating arts institutions to renew a downtown area. Asheville, North Carolina created a similar complex, although with somewhat less success (possibly because they didn't sufficiently modify the model to fit local conditions). In these times, when funding for the arts is more of a struggle than ever, the Center model might well provide a way to support the cultural and educational initiatives of local cultural institutions, while creating new destinations in urban centers.

Sustaining Urban Excellence

The 1997 Selection Committee emphasized the importance of sustainability as a critical element in urban excellence. While the creative and innovative visions developed by the 1997 winners have the potential to make important contributions to urban placemaking, much of that potential is lost if a project cannot sustain itself over time. In its investigation into the longevity of urban excellence, (see *Sustaining Urban Excellence: Learning from the Rudy Bruner Award 1987-1993*, Bruner Foundation, 1998), the Bruner Foundation has identified a number of factors critical to long-term success

Financial Independence

Financial stability can derive from something as basic as predictable cash flow and capital reserves to more complex financial mechanisms, such as the sale of historic preservation tax credits. In order to provide stability, sources of cash must be free from fluctuations of financial markets or political trends. **The Times Square** is in the enviable position of having been generously funded for acquisition and construction, leaving a significant capital reserve which protects the project from unforeseen city operating budget cuts. Its operating expenses are covered by rents, while the extensive social services are financed by contracts with the state, and job training is financed by the high-rent retail operations this location can command. This diversified set of funding sources, together with its cash reserve, give The Times Square an unusually strong financial outlook.

Emily Axelrod, Director of the Rudy Bruner Award, with Josh Simon of Hismen Hin-Nu and Simeon Bruner, Founder of the Rudy Bruner Award

Center in the Square bases its operating budget on contributions from various governmental agencies, including the state, city, and county, and is looking to create a substantial endowment through fundraising. The variety of supporting jurisdictions adds stability to its funding sources. However, sudden changes in the funding patterns of the state, county or city, could conceivably put Center in the Square at risk, but the contribution made by the project to educational opportunity in the area gives it an advantageous position with respect to public funding. As long as the educational and cultural benefits continue to be perceived as valuable, funding is likely to remain secure.

The prospects for sustainability for **Hismen Hin-nu** are excellent. Permanent financing for both the residential and commercial portions of the project have been provided by a combination of state and local entities, as well as by EBALDC itself. The rent structure allows the project to operate within budget, and to make regular payments on its remaining debt. The developer, EBALDC, is a financially secure and mature community development organization, adding another level of financial security to the project. There is no reason to believe that Hismen Hin-nu faces financial instability, despite retail vacancies.

Project Row Houses has relied on very different types of financing to develop its programs. Many of its most important funding sources are one-time grants and loans from private individuals and foundations. Project Row Houses is well aware that renewable, ongoing funding sources will be critical to its future. Its Board is actively involved in fundraising for the project, with the goal of acquiring additional assets in the form of adjacent property, and securing a source of endowment capital sufficient to ensure a predictable cash flow. In addition, Project Row Houses is working hard to develop an improved relationship with Houston's Department of Community Development, which could be helpful to the project's future.

Sustainability of the **Cleveland Historic Warehouse District** is far more complex. Each renovation project within the district must create its own financial package. The viability of individual projects depends upon the health of the local economy, the cost of borrowing money, and the availability of financial incentives such as low income tax credits, historic conservation easements, property tax abatements, and other mechanisms which provide significant public subsidies. Currently the prospect of ongoing availability of these tools is very positive, as the City of Cleveland has become a supporter of development of the district.

Leadership Transition

The first section of this chapter discusses the importance of the vision of a strong and capable leader. However talented and visionary these leaders may be, however, the future of the places they create will depend upon their ability to introduce, train, and gain support for new generations of leaders who will carry their projects into the future. They need to develop resilient organizations that are able to adapt to inevitable changes in leadership.

At **The Times Square**, Rosanne Haggerty is the symbol and personification of the project. It was her vision and skill that persuaded the City of New York to grant to Common Ground the largest award of its kind ever given in New York City. Her total commitment to the project from its inception has been critical to its success.

Today, however, Haggerty is less involved in the daily operations of the project and is devoting more time to adapting The Times Square model to new projects. New staff have been hired and are being trained to take over the management role, while she remains available to ensure consistency with the philosophy and mission that guided the establishment of the project. Leadership transition is well underway and shows every sign of proceeding smoothly.

Project Row Houses has been closely linked with the energy and vision of its founder, Rick Lowe. Lowe recognized early that it was critical to bring on an executive director (Grotfeldt) to broaden the base of leadership for Project Row Houses and contribute needed day-to-day management skills. While both Lowe and Grotfeldt remain committed to Project Row Houses, they are also involved in other initiatives throughout the country. Training new leadership to run day-to-day operations is an ongoing effort, and will be important to the future success of the project. Project Row Houses has not yet attained a degree of stability which would withstand the absence of its original leaders; thus, it is still important for them to remain closely involved at home.

Projects like **Cleveland Historic Warehouse District**, **Hismen Hin-nu,** and **Center in the Square**, are run by mature organizations, which have already experienced changes in leadership and personnel. They have passed the initial stage of vision and creation which are characteristic of newer projects, and now require seasoned and capable managers. As a result these places are far less dependent upon key individuals for long term stability. There is every reason to assume that these projects can withstand future leadership transitions as long as care is taken to choose leaders who remain committed to the original project values.

Conclusion

The 1997 Rudy Bruner Award winners reflect several important truths about urban placemaking, and address some of the most critical issues facing our cities today. As a group, they provide us with new models of urban excellence that can be adapted to cities and neighborhoods across the country. As individual projects, they demonstrate creative solutions to local urban problems — solutions which are built on the cornerstones of the Rudy Bruner Award: **process, place,** and **values.**

The 1997 winners have enriched and enlivened their cities and their neighborhoods, and made a lasting contribution to the urban environment. They have provided new models of urban excellence, and have demonstrated once again what can be accomplished through imagination, dedication, and hard work. "Change in cities," one Selection Committee member said, "is often attributable to a couple of people who do something, and everything spins around it. And… often it's something you figure can't actually be done, but they do it anyway."